TALES
from the Igloo

Edited and translated by Father Maurice Metayer
Foreword by Al Purdy
Illustrated by Agnes Nanogak

ST. MARTIN'S PRESS NEW YORK
ST. JAMES PRESS LONDON

Copyright © 1972 by Maurice Métayer
St. Martin's Press, Inc. 175 Fifth Ave., New York, N.Y. 10010
Printed in Canada
Library of Congress Catalog Card Number: 76-54253
First published in the United States of America in 1977

ISBN-312-78418-X

Library of Congress Cataloging in Publication Data

Métayer, Maurice.
    Tales from the igloo.

    CONTENTS: The magic drum.—Kajortoq, the red fox.—
The orphan and the bears.—The ball players [etc.]
    1. Eskimos—Canada—Northwest Territories—Legends.
I. Title.
E99.E7M5313   1977   398.2   76-54253

St. James Press
3 Percy Street
London W1P 9FA

Printed and bound in Canada

Contents

Foreword

The first story in this book is called "The Magic Drum." It tells about a girl who rejected all offers of marriage, had her flesh devoured by "sea animals" and became a "walking skeleton." Everyone is afraid of her and runs away, except one useless old man. The skeleton girl and the old man become friends; she has him fashion a drum, a magic drum, which has the power of replacing her lost flesh as well as making the old man young once again. Of course the two become man and wife, and presumably no longer outsiders from their own people.

Father Metayer interprets this myth for me in a letter: "The girl of the story did not want to be loved by any of the young men of her group. Because she rejected love, her beauty, her very flesh, was destroyed. Only when somebody loved her . . . when she accepted him, was she 'born again' as a beautiful girl. And in turn her love gave back to the old man his lost youth.

"You see now the very important message of this story: a woman is not fully a woman without the love of a man. And a man will never grow old as long as he has the love of a woman."

When you read this particular story, that interpretation may seem didactic: as Father Metayer says, these myths amount to advice for future generations about how to live a life to best advantage. But the myth itself is not didactic before interpretation.

An old shaman/storyteller in an ancient igloo or a modern prefab house, face shining like a television set, says to his audience: "Here's an interesting story. It's a lot of fun and you'll enjoy it." On second thought, he probably doesn't say that, for his audience knows it without such introductory remarks. But the stories *are* fun; after the long passage of time, fact and legend merge and become myth.

Of course a great deal of time has passed, and the Eskimo environment has changed, since the early period during which these myths came into being. Rifles have replaced harpoons and spears, snowmobiles supplanted dog teams for the most part, canvas tents and prefabs succeed igloos and whalebone houses. We all know this to be true if we follow the current trend of oil and mining operations in the north and their sometimes ruination of the Arctic ecology, of the blue-roofed outdoor living room Eskimos have occupied for centuries.

But some things have not changed; among them, human character. People in these myths are implicitly both human and animal. If we read the stories as morality tales only—since we know a few of them are just that—then they change shape before the eye and ear and become fairy tales without apparent meaning. I think the best way to listen to all these marvellous things—bear into man and man into bear—is for their own surface interest and for the marvels of a strange cold and warm country that is the Canadian northern backyard.

In some sense I see the Eskimos of these myths as pragmatic traditionalists. (And here I'm succumbing to the pitfall of interpretation, which I ought to sternly resist.) Their physical world is snow and ice of winter, the blue sky-vaulted blaze of flowers in a briefly comfortable summer. The good guy wins, the bad guy loses, except that there are no labels to help you figure out which is which. It is a world already in being, for there are no prefatory creation myths here, no all-seeing omnipotent gods to influence the future. A closed world.

But turn from the myths to the drawings that illustrate them. Looking at them I feel as if I've entered a child's world, everyone enthralled by a magic spell. But the children here act like adults, as they are quickly forced to be by the northern environment. (In a somewhat different child's world, watching Japanese samurai soap operas last year, I saw wizards leap fifty feet straight up in the air before the eyes of astonished officials, making strange "urrr-ur-ur" sounds in their throats. I was just as astonished and enthralled. The child's world and that of Japanese and Eskimo wizards merge.) Terrible things happen in this contiguous world to reality, although generally for reasons of food and survival. Death itself is sometimes circumvented and unreal.

Years ago I read books about the Arctic: red-mouthed polar bears and lovable seals cavorted on the ice floes; kayaks paddled by brown hunters roamed the seas; icy igloos glowed at night like white sunsets from oil lamps within. When I actually visited the Arctic in 1965, it was overlaid with the myths that I had read about. Reality with the super-real seen beyond an almost palpable veil, from which the rays of another sun and moon sometimes reached out. If you turn this book at just the right angle of vision and belief, you may catch a glimpse of that world.

AL PURDY
Ameliasburg
Ontario

Preface

The tales told here are those of a group of Inuit people known to ethnologists as the Copper Eskimos.

This Eskimo people live mainly between 103 degrees and 123 degrees west longitude, an area that extends at one point south of the Arctic Circle to Taherjuaq (Contwoyto) Lake. Their settlements are found primarily along the shores of the Arctic Ocean and on the islands immediately to the north of the mainland. The severe climatic conditions that characterize this region contributed to the relative isolation of these people from *qablunat*, or "the men of thick eyebrows," as the Inuit call the white race. Brief navigational seasons meant that Inuit and *qablunat* met infrequently.

However the Copper Eskimos had periodic contact with groups of Indian people living in the area immediately south of the Inuit territory. Friendly meetings and occasional bartering typified these encounters but open conflict was not unknown. The Indian people ventured north in quest of raw copper, a resource which the Eskimo people also exploited. It was in the course of one of these expeditions, in 1771 at Bloody Falls, a few miles from the mouth of the Coppermine River, that Samuel Hearne's Indian guides massacred an entire settlement of sleeping Inuit people.

There were contacts with other explorers as well: Franklin in 1821, Dease and Simpson in 1839, Richardson and Rae in 1848, Stefansson in 1910, the Canadian Expedition of 1913-18, and the Danes of the Fifth Thule Expedition in 1923.

The art of storytelling must have followed closely the evolution of language. As soon as our ancestors were able to understand that they had a past and that they should transmit it to their children, myths and legends made their appearance, impressing upon the youngest of the race the physical and spiritual experiences of the eldest.

Before writing was invented this was a purely oral exchange, no doubt accompanied by rituals which symbolically revived the past. To give an object or being a name is to grant it existence; to narrate one's experiences is to share them with all.

The Sumerians knew how to express their experiences in written symbols at least thirty-five hundred years ago, but many other cultures were without writing until relatively few years ago. The Inuit were one of these peoples.

In terms of passing on their history, culture and traditions, the Copper Eskimo people relied solely on oral transmission. The legends in this collection have come down through their generations in such a fashion. Through the lips of the Inuit have been transmitted those phenomena seen and heard of, understood and remembered without the help of the written word.

Most often it was at night in the igloo, during the long winter evenings, that the old storytellers passed on legends of the past to the younger people. With a few taps of a stick one of the women extinguished the greater part of the wick of the stone lamp. A few flames still danced but gave little illumination. In this uncertain light the dome and the walls of the igloo became vague forms, dissolving the confines of the igloo as if the darkness of the night had entered. Each individual was in direct communion with the infinite Arctic country, with its oceans and land, with its mountains, its mystery. Each imagination was stirred.

No one was asleep in the igloo but each was on the verge of dreams. The voice of the storyteller rekindled the flames of the past while the present disappeared. It was the age of the ancestors that became reality and one relived the lives of heroes and performed heroic feats. Everyone grasped some significance in the story, everyone understood to the extent of his own fears and hopes.

The expert in the science of mythology will make a structural analysis of the myth in order to arrive at its true meaning. However, at the point of original transmission in the igloo, the Inuit listener would arrive instinctively at its meaning, hidden though it may be under the trappings of the story, and thereby find satisfying answers to the mysteries of his world.

In gathering these legends the following method was adopted: first they were recorded on tape; each story was analyzed to obtain an exact translation. This translation in turn served as the basis for French and English texts. On occasion the text as it appears here departs from the literal translation in the interests of adhering to the style of the English and French languages. Yet the smallest detail of Inuit thought has been faithfully respected.

collection: Helen Qalvakadlak, Louis Qajuina, James Qavviaktoq, James Qoer-huk, Effie Qarqajaq and Fred Atātakhaq provided the original taped material.

Following completion of the text the legends were placed in the hands of the artists of the Holman Island Cooperative. Agnes Nanogak has provided her interpretation of each legend through the medium of coloured drawings.

Several other people have helped to make this publication possible. It would have been difficult to do the work well without the understanding and assistance of S. M. Hodgson, Commissioner of the Northwest Territories. To Mr. R. McNeely and especially to Mrs. M. McNeely gratitude is expressed for their assistance in preparing the English text. And to the staff of the Curriculum Division of the Northwest Territories' Department of Education, deepest thanks are extended, especially to Paul Robinson, chief of the Division, who read and edited the complete text and suggested many improvements which have been retained.

MAURICE METAYER, O.M.I.
Cambridge Bay
Northwest Territories

The Magic Drum

An old married couple had a daughter who did not want to marry. It was not that she lacked suitors; young men who were good hunters had come from great distances to take her for their wife. But she had refused all proposals. She had said no to all. To all, that is, but the last two brothers who had come.

These brothers arrived with the same intentions as the others. When first they entered the igloo the girl took them to be men just like their predecessors. However, though they had neither said nor done anything extraordinary, the girl became attracted to them.

She followed them outside the igloo. Scarcely were they outside when the two brothers reclothed themselves in the skins which they had left at the door. The young woman then recognized them for what they were—white bears.

They took her away over the ice and forced her to descend into the water through a hole in the ice. For some time she was dragged along through the water, only to be abandoned when the bears came to another opening through which they disappeared.

Left on her own, the girl sank to the floor of the ocean. When her feet touched bottom she was able to look about her. One side of the ocean appeared to be darker, the opposite side seemed brighter. She reasoned that the dark side must lie to the north so she began to walk toward the south where the light was brighter.

While she was walking tiny sea animals surrounded her. They bit into her body, tearing away strips of flesh. Little by little her body was devoured. Eventually only her bones remained. Then she noticed an unusually bright area which led her to think that she was about to find a place where she could climb up to the land. She was nothing but a skeleton but resolutely she advanced toward the light. She found a crevasse in the ice and was able to climb up onto the ice surface.

Having come this far she began to reflect on her past. In her mind's eye she saw her parents with their well-filled storeroom and she asked herself what she must do to have the same. While pondering this problem she took some snow and made a small igloo, one that resembled that of her father. She also built a small platform as a storage place.

When she had finished, she thought out loud: "I have nothing warm in which to sleep. I need a sleeping bag, some skins and some furs." With these thoughts she fell asleep.

On awakening, the woman was surprised to see a big igloo, exactly like her father's, in front of her own. Near it lay a freshly killed caribou. Her dreams had been realized! She dried the caribou hide and made herself a sleeping bag. The meat she prepared for storage on the platform.

From that time on, each night before going to sleep, she would think of what she needed, knowing that when she awoke the next day everything would be provided. In this manner she soon had all she required, except her own flesh. What the sea animals had eaten could not be replaced. She remained a walking skeleton.

Each day she spent long periods of time on the ice. On one such occasion she happened to see hunters coming down to the sea ice to hunt seals. The young woman wanted to meet these people and talk to them. But when she approached them the hunters fled in fear. Disappointed, the girl watched them disappear into the distance. Then she returned to her igloo thinking: "I would like to have met them, but I frightened them. It is I who prevented them from coming. I am but a skeleton and my bones clatter when I walk. No doubt they were afraid of me; that is why they ran." She was sad and began to torment herself because she had been unable to get close to the hunters.

The father of these hunters was an old man and when his sons had gone to hunt at the sea he had been left behind. They had made him stay in his igloo; he was no longer capable of hunting and could not provide himself with anything to eat.

Upon his sons' return they told their father: "Yesterday we saw a woman who was nothing but a skeleton. She came to meet us, but we were afraid. We fled and did not see her again."

"Ah, well," replied the old man, "I don't have much longer to live. I shall go and meet her tomorrow."

The next morning the old man went to find the girl and found her sitting in the entrance of her igloo. She did not move towards him, but when he arrived she invited him to enter the igloo. The interior was bright with the light from the stone lamps. They ate and then went to sleep.

When morning came, the girl who had been reduced to a skeleton spoke to the old man who was no longer able to hunt.

"Make me a drum," she said. "Make me a very small drum." The old man immediately went to work to satisfy her desire. When he finished he gave her the instrument. The woman blew out the lamps, took the drum and began to dance. She beat the drum with a stick while repeating a magic incantation. The drum grew larger and the sound of the beat swelled and seemed to fill the air.

The dance finished, the lamps were relit and the old man was once more able to see the girl. To his amazement the skeleton had gone; instead a pretty young girl, dressed in superb clothing, appeared before him.

The girl took the drum again, blew out the lamps, and began to dance. After a while she asked her visitor, "Are you all right like that?" With his affirmative reply she relit the lamps. It was no longer an old man who appeared before her, but rather a handsome young man. The magic rhythm of the drum had given him back his youth.

This is how the girl who had not wanted to marry and who had been eaten by the beasts of the sea found a husband.

When they returned to the old man's family no one recognized him. His own sons said, "Our father, who is very old has travelled north toward the sea and has not returned."

"I am your father," replied the man. "I was once old and this woman was but a skeleton. However, we have both become young and handsome and now she is my wife."

Kajortoq, the Red Fox

One summer day, Kajortoq, the red fox, left her brood of cubs in the den and went out in search of something to eat. On a vast plain she met Aklaq, the brown bear, and said: "Cousin, it has been a long time since I last saw you! What is the matter with you?"

"I am hungry," replied Aklaq.

"Me too. I really am," said Kajortoq. "Let's hunt together. You go this way and I shall go that way."

"There is nothing this way but ptarmigan," complained Aklaq, "and they are afraid of me. Every time I get close to them they fly away."

"It is easy for me to catch them," remarked the fox. "But," she added, "I am afraid of men."

"I am not afraid of men," said Aklaq, "but I am unable to catch ptarmigan."

"In that case," declared Kajortoq, "wait for me here; I shall go and get you some ptarmigan. I shall not be long."

Aklaq waited and Kajortoq soon returned with a few ptarmigan. The brown bear was full of joy and thanked his companion again and again. He was very hungry and ate the ptarmigan at once. When he had finished he said, "You were very kind to bring me some ptarmigan. In return I shall now bring you a man. Wait for me here."

Kajortoq waited but the bear took a long time to return, and when he did arrive he had no man. Instead he staggered along; he was losing blood and

behind him the ground was red. A man had shot an arrow at him and had wounded him in the side. The shaft of the arrow had broken and the point remained in the flesh.

Kajortoq sympathized: "Cousin, I feel sorry for you. Let me take care of you." Kajortoq built a stone fireplace, lit a fire, and heated some stones.

"Stretch out here," she told the bear. "Stretch your legs and even if I hurt you, do not move. If you stir, you will die because I shall not be able to remove the arrow."

The bear stretched out on the ground. The fox took a red hot stone from the fire and applied it to the wound pushing harder and harder on it. Aklaq moaned and howled with pain, but soon the howls stopped; he was dead.

Kajortoq stood on her hind legs and danced around the bear, laughing loudly: "I can brag to myself. No one could do this but I. I have enough to eat for a long time." The fox did not return to her lair but remained at this place for the duration of the summer, feeding herself on the meat of the bear.

When winter came she had run out of provisions. The bear had all been eaten; there was nothing left but the bones. She placed them in a pile and buried them under some boulders.

A while later she saw Amaroq, the wolf, coming toward her and went to meet him. "How are you, cousin?"

"Not too well," answered Amaroq, "I am very hungry."

"Have confidence in me," said Kajortoq. "I shall show you what you have to do to get some food. Do you see that river in front of us?" She pointed to a nearby river covered with a thin coating of ice. Here and there water could be seen through holes in the ice.

"Go over there," suggested Kajortoq. "Try to catch some trout. I am going to make you a fish hook. All you have to do is sit near the hole, tie the hook to your tail and let it sink to the bottom. Remain seated and do not move until the sun sets. At that time you will pull in your hook. There will be a trout caught on it. Believe me, that is how I caught mine."

The wolf sat beside the hole without moving. Meanwhile, the red fox set out along the shore saying that she was going to look for something to eat. Instead she hid behind a small hill to watch the wolf, but being careful that he not see her.

Amaroq stayed where he was for the entire day, confidently awaiting the results of his fishing. By the time the sun had reached the west he realized he had caught nothing. He growled in anger, "Kajortoq lied to me. I am going to run after her and eat her!"

He tried to get up but his tail was stuck to the ice. He pulled on it again and again until all of a sudden it came free; his tail had broken. Frothing with rage and bleeding profusely, the wolf searched the plain for traces of Kajortoq. The fox, however, had slipped away to hide in her hole.

The wolf soon discovered her den and cried, "Come out of your hole so that I can eat you!"

"What are you saying?" answered Kajortoq, sticking her head out of her den to look. As she did so she bent her head to one side and kept one of her eyes closed. "I have never seen you before. What do you want?"

"You deceived me today and I have lost my tail. Now I am going to eat you!"

"I know nothing about that," replied Kajortoq emerging from her hole. "Did you ask that red fox over there? It must be him. I heard someone pass my door a little while ago."

Impatiently, the wolf left Kajortoq to run after the other red fox. Kajortoq saw him go and kept watching until the wolf fell from his wound. By the next morning, having lost all of his blood, Amaroq was dead. Kajortoq stood up on her hind legs and started dancing in circles around him. "I can boast to myself. No one could do this but I."

She lived on the wolf all of that winter. When she had eaten all his flesh, she made a pile of the bones and went elsewhere in search of food.

One day she saw coming toward her a brown female bear who looked larger and more terrifying than any bear Kajortoq had ever seen.

The bear addressed the fox angrily. "Did you know my son? He left last spring to hunt but he did not come back. I have found his bones near this hill."

"I know nothing about it," answered Kajortoq. "I did not see him. I shall follow you and you can show me where his bones are."

They left together. The fox recognized the place where she had killed Aklaq. Seeing that the female bear was crying Kajortoq pretended to be full of sorrow.

"Tears won't help you," she told the mother bear. "I believe I know who killed your son. Wait here awhile for me."

Kajortoq climbed to the top of a hill. From this vantage point she looked in all directions and saw another brown bear. She returned in haste to the female bear and said, "The one who killed your son is over there. Go and attack him. He is big and strong but I shall help you."

While the bears fought Kajortoq jumped around pretending to help. In fact, she only spattered blood on her hair. At length the female bear killed the other bear. She turned to the fox and said gratefully, "You helped me, thank you. Take all this meat. I am tired and wounded and do not want any of it." The bear started homeward, but died of her wounds before she was out of sight.

Kajortoq once again danced for joy and was happy. The two bears would provide plenty of meat for a long time to come.

The Orphan and the Bears

Near the mouth of a river lived a group of hunters. Their igloos were located in such a way that the men had easy access to both the sea ice where the seals were to be found, and to the surrounding hills where the caribou grazed.

One day a group of men went in search of the caribou. They left the settlement in their kayaks and travelled many miles up the river. They did not return. Eventually, a second group of hunters set out to search for the missing men. They, too, did not return. The people remaining in the settlement were uncertain as to what they should do. They were afraid that even more of their hunters might be lost.

It happened that living amongst the people was a young orphan boy. Possessing few personal belongings he had often dreamed of owning a kayak and of being a great hunter. When he learned that a number of the hunters of his settlement had not returned from the hunt, the young boy thought that perhaps he could go in search of the missing men. He decided to ask the most important hunter if he could borrow his kayak and search for those who were lost.

The older man cautioned him. "If you leave there is a chance that you too might never return. However, if you are willing to take this risk my kayak and harpoon are there at the bank of the river. You may take them."

The boy was overjoyed. Quickly he set out, heading up the river. As he travelled he used the harpoon to keep himself supplied with food. Ducks and other birds were plentiful. His aim was so accurate that he was able to kill them as they were flying overhead. In this manner the boy made good progress.

After some time he sighted some large igloos close to the bank of the river. "That's strange," he thought. "I have never heard that people were living here. Can it be that these are the igloos of the missing men? Perhaps they are being held captive here and are forbidden to leave this place." The boy paddled his kayak toward the shore in order to take a closer look.

Situated close by the river was a huge igloo. Considering the possibility that the hunters might be held prisoner there, the boy swung his kayak into the shore, jumped out, and cautiously made his way toward this igloo. With him he took his harpoon and the birds which he had killed.

No one was in sight as he climbed up the bank. Entering the igloo he found it deserted. Not knowing quite what to do, the boy sat down inside the igloo for a brief rest. While he was pondering his next move he happened to notice an opening in the igloo wall. What appeared to be a window was located high up the wall, halfway to the dome of the igloo.

A moment later he heard the sound of someone approaching. Glancing upward he saw something through the window-like opening. All he could make out was a large mouth asking for something to eat. Without hesitation the boy threw one of the ducks that he had killed through this opening. In an instant the face at the window snatched the duck and disappeared.

The boy remained in the igloo. Frightened though he was, he had recognized the hungry visitor. It was a bear-man. Many times the boy had heard stories of these beasts who lived in igloos like people and who could take off their outer skins whenever they were inside their own homes. When they were out hunting the bear-men wore their skins and were very, very dangerous.

After a short absence the bear-man returned. The young hunter once again saw the menacing mouth in the opening. For a second time the boy threw one of his remaining ducks to the beast. The bear-man left, but only to return again and again until finally the boy had used up his entire food supply. The next time the face appeared at the window there would be nothing left to give him.

The boy felt trapped. "Without doubt this is what happened to the hunters I am searching for," he thought. "They, too, likely ran out of food and thus were killed by these bear-men. My only hope is my harpoon!"

The next time the beast appeared the boy was ready. Taking careful aim he threw the harpoon with all his might. The weapon found its mark, penetrating deeply into the body of the bear-man. The boy held on to the harpoon line pulling as hard as he could, but the line broke; the beast was still alive and the boy was defenceless.

Realizing that he was in grave danger the boy fled the igloo. He feared that the parents of the beast that had been wounded would come looking for him. Outside the igloo the boy spotted another dwelling nearby. It was much smaller than the first. He ran to it and without bothering to knock at the door immediately ducked inside.

Here he found two old bear-women lying on the bed. Without hesitating the boy fell upon them and killed them both. Working feverishly, he took one of the slain bear-women and propped her up in bed as if she were asleep. The other one he began to skin. As soon as the skinning was completed, he hid the body under the bed and dressed himself in the hide of his victim.

No sooner was this done than he heard footsteps approaching. One by one the bear-men entered the igloo. "Our great hunter in the igloo nearby has been wounded," they said. "There is something stuck in his body. He is suffering greatly. Come and take care of him."

The boy, pretending to be the old bear-woman that he had just killed, replied, "I can no longer walk. I have lost my strength. My companion has fallen asleep but do not wake her. She needs her rest." The bear-men insisted, "We shall lift you by the arms and carry you to the igloo. Our great hunter will not live long if you do not help. Come quickly!"

The young man, dressed in the bearskin, slowly rose to his feet, imitating as he did so the trembling of an old bear-woman. The bear-men helped him to the door. Slowly they dragged him toward the other igloo. Try as he might the young boy was not able to act out the part of the old bear-woman entirely. The bear-men grew suspicious. "How is it you appear to be stronger than usual?" they asked.

"It is because I am trying with all my powers to walk," replied the boy. "It may seem to you that I am stronger than I really am." The bear-men asked no further questions.

Once inside the other igloo the boy saw the wounded beast lying in the middle of the floor. He looked about for a long, sharp stone which he began to heat over the flame of the stone lamp. As he did so he told the bear-men what had to be done.

"I am going to remove the harpoon from the great hunter's body. While I am doing so, you are to blow out the lamp, turn around and face the wall and make as much noise as possible." This they did.

The boy set to work. First, he grabbed the end of the broken harpoon line and tried to withdraw the weapon. As before, the strap broke. Next he took the sharp stone which had been heated and with it made a sharp gash in the beast's flesh around the head of the harpoon. The weapon came free. Into the gaping wound he plunged the hot stone. The great hunter howled in pain, but the other bear-men could not hear. They were making too much noise and had their backs turned to their wounded friend.

The boy knew what he had to do. He shed his bearskin, picked up his harpoon and ran as fast as he could toward his kayak. Without stopping he jumped into his kayak and paddled furiously. The bear-men, realizing that they had been tricked, tried to pursue him. Their efforts were in vain. Whenever they got close to the kayak the young hunter would brandish his harpoon and scare them away. Finally, they gave up the chase.

When the boy returned to his settlement he repeated the story of his adventures. The people now knew what had happened to the missing men. The great hunter who had loaned the boy his kayak and harpoon was satisfied with what the boy had done and from that time on the young boy was cared for by this man.

The Ball Players

Two groups of people lived across a river from one another. Every now and then some of the men met to play ball, those from one side of the river against those from the other side.

The same team always won and as soon as they arrived home in their kayaks they would shout and laugh with joy. In the losers' camp unhappiness and frustration prevailed.

One day, after being defeated in yet another game, an older man on the losing team took the ball used in the game and cast a spell upon it. He was certain that the winners across the river would soon be back for another game so he performed a magic rite that would make the ball disappear.

In the game that subsequently took place, the men had hardly begun to play when the ball disappeared. No one knew where to find it. The visitors recrossed the river, very unhappy at having lost the ball which had brought them such luck.

The man who had caused the ball to vanish used his magic once again. When all were sleeping in the victors' camp a curse was laid upon the ball players among them. The next morning, when these men left their tents to inspect the weather, they immediately fell to the ground. They were dead.

Joy now spread through the losers' settlement and their men, descending the river in quest of seals, cried out in triumph. They had been victorious even without the use of a ball.

Meanwhile, in the settlement where death had come, one of the surviving men devised a means of winning revenge. He took a loon and skinned it very carefully so as not to damage the skin in any way. Then he stuffed it with dried herbs and took it outdoors where he stood it in an upright position. All the while he was angrily contemplating those who had killed his relatives and friends.

On checking his magic loon a while later, this man noticed that frost was beginning to form on the down around the beak of the bird, as if it were beginning to breathe a little. To look at its feathers one would have thought that the bird was alive.

More time passed before the man came out to look at his creation again. This time the loon was no longer there. It had come to life and flown away.

Those across the river had gone seal hunting toward the north and after a time returned home. They were already on the return journey when a loon suddenly appeared in the water ahead of their kayaks. The men were about to harpoon the bird when it made a sudden dive. The men in the kayak nearest to the spot where the loon had disappeared headed in that direction only to discover an immense whirlpool in their path. Their kayak was soon caught in the turbulent water, whirling them around and around until they were dragged down into the center of the funnel. The kayak disappeared beneath the water.

From the river bank their adversaries had watched everything. They had again won and had taken their revenge with the aid of the magic loon. It was their turn to rejoice in victory.

Kautaluk

Living on the Arctic coast among a group of Inuit people were an old woman and her grandson, Kautaluk. As the parents of the young boy were both dead, there was no one to hunt for them. Sometimes kind people would give them food, but more often than not they had to make do with other people's leftovers.

Although some people respected Kautaluk and his grandmother, there were others who tried to make their lives miserable. With no one strong enough to protect him, Kautaluk often found himself being teased and tormented. On occasions when he would visit the igloos of these people, they would catch him by the nose and lift him off his feet. At times like these Kautaluk endured terrible pain. When he was very hungry the same people would offer him only scraps of food.

One night after Kautaluk returned home suffering from this cruel treatment, he received a visitor. All was peaceful and still in the settlement when the Great Spirit that watches over the earth came to Kautaluk and gave him the gift of great strength. Kautaluk told no one of what had happened. Instead, he proceeded to try out his newly acquired powers. While everyone was sleeping he went outside and began to pick up the most enormous boulders he could find. One by one he threw them toward the igloos where his tormentors slept. Later Kautaluk found a huge tree that had been washed ashore by the ocean waves. This he carried to the door of the igloo of one of his worst persecutors.

The following morning when the people came out of their homes they were amazed to see the rocks and the tree trunk.

"How could this have happened?" they wondered. "No human being could possibly have done this to us." Kautaluk said nothing.

Sometime thereafter, Kautaluk was visited once again. This time the Great Spirit told him, "A white bear and her two cubs will arrive soon. Their skins will make a warm sleeping bag for the two of you." At that time Kautaluk and his grandmother had nothing with which to cover themselves in their icy igloo. Only the warmth of his grandmother's body had kept Kautaluk from freezing while he slept.

It was not long after that one of the hunters spotted a mother bear and her two cubs. All of the men immediately ran out onto the ice. Kautaluk watched the hunters as they ran past him. Then he took his grandmother's boots, laced them up and set out in the direction of the bears. Running quickly, Kautaluk soon caught up with and then passed all of the other hunters. He wanted to get to the bears first.

The men were astonished to recognize Kautaluk passing them by. With one voice they declared, "Oh, that is only Kautaluk. Surely he will be attacked and bitten. That poor orphan, running about in his grandmother's boots! He will be killed!"

Kautaluk paid no attention. He ran directly toward the bears and grasping them by the hind legs, he repeatedly beat them on the ice like a woman knocking snow out of clothing. The three bears were quickly killed. This done, Kautaluk picked up the bears and effortlessly carried them back to his grandmother's igloo. The hunters meekly followed him.

Arriving at the igloo Kautaluk turned back to the men and said, "There is food here for us all, but first you must skin the bears. My grandmother and I shall make fine sleeping bags from their hides." The hunters set to work without comment.

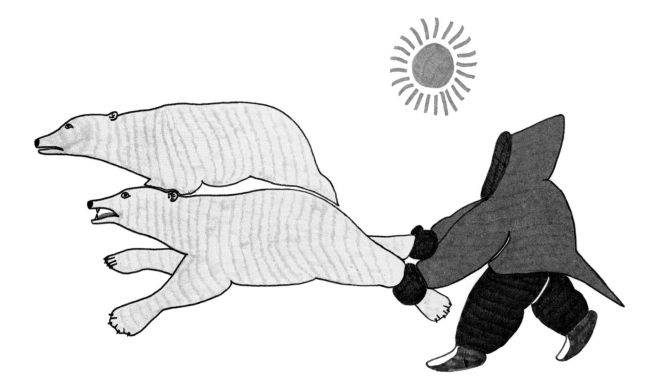

When the skinning was completed, Kautaluk gave each man some meat for his family. The wives could now begin the cooking in their large pots over the open fires.

As was his custom Kautaluk went around the settlement visiting each igloo in turn. In every one there was plenty of meat to eat. Unlike previous visits everyone invited him to eat with them. Only the choicest, most delicious parts of the bear were offered to him. Kautaluk refused this generosity saying, "I have never eaten these succulent pieces before. Just give me a part of the tough end. I only wish to eat those parts to which I am accustomed."

Having won the admiration of many of the people, it was not long before Kautaluk wanted to have his own home. He wished to take a wife. He chose for his wife the daughter of his greatest tormentor! He wanted the girl, but he did not wish to have anything to do with her father. He decided that one last time he would demonstrate his strength for all to see. In this way he could be certain that people would never treat him unfairly again.

When everyone was asleep Kautaluk quietly walked about the settlement. Finding another large tree that had been thrown up on the shore, he carried it to the igloo which belonged to the girl's father. Carefully, he balanced the tree against the igloo in such a way that unless he himself removed it, the slightest movement from the people within would cause the tree to crash through the walls crushing everyone inside. Throughout the night Kautaluk proceeded to do the same thing to the igloos of all of those who had mistreated him.

The following day fear and panic spread through the settlement. The people made ready to leave this place for their lives were obviously in danger.

Kautaluk then revealed his tremendous strength by removing the trees from the igloos of his former enemies. All of the people were awe-struck and his persecutors feared for their lives. Preparations were made to leave.

However, to those who had been kind to him, Kautaluk called out, "You do not have to go. You helped me when I was weak. Stay here and my grandmother and my wife and I will stay here with you." And so they did.

The Owl and the Ptarmigan

Ukpik, the big owl of the Arctic desert, was in love with Aqilgieq, the little white ptarmigan. However Aqilgieq already had a husband whom she loved very much.

In a fit of jealousy, Ukpik killed his rival and began to woo Aqilgieq in the hope of winning her heart. But the little ptarmigan cried for her dead husband; she did not love her new suitor and began to sing a song of ridicule:

"Ukpik, go away!
With your big head
And your too large eyes
And your sorry-looking legs—
You are ugly!
Who would want you for a husband?
Who would want for a husband
A being like you?
With big knitted eyebrows,
With lashes that long,
You big dumpy owl,
With no feet and no neck!"

Ukpik, who thought himself handsome, became angry and wanted to shame Aqilgieq in return and so he sang:

"Eater of owls! Bah!
I shall leave you!"
So saying, he flew away.

The Swan and the Crane

A swan was walking along the edge of a lake looking for those places where plants grow tall and thick. He found a field of downy plants sprinkled with white wisps and so stopped there to eat. A female crane flew by overhead and began circling about him, trying to attract his attention. Diving towards the swan she filled his ears with the whistling sound of her wings.

The swan lifted his head in appreciation and winked invitingly. The crane answered by executing a dance in her flight, beating her wings so that the swan would keep his eyes on her.

The swan followed her with his eyes and said, "You certainly are lively! Come and rest here beside me. Come play with me."

"What kind of games?" asked the crane. "Do you want us to dance?"

The swan answered that he was a terrible dancer. "However," he added, "we can play by pulling each other by the neck. We shall see which one of us has the stronger neck."

"All right," agreed the crane as she landed in the field near the swan.

The two birds prepared themselves. Standing face to face they entwined their necks and each started to pull away from the other. Slowly but surely, the crane pulled her opponent's neck toward the ground.

The swan saw that he would be unable to prevent himself from falling. With all his strength he gave a violent tug in order to regain his balance. But this sudden effort completely exhausted the swan; his neck was now limp and he fell over backward!

An instant later he was back on his feet eyeing the crane. The crane began singing her song of victory.

"There is nothing solid in a swan's neck,
Whereas mine is well built!
Confess that you fell backward
Without being able to stop yourself!"

The swan had been thinking over a few lines of his own. He could not let the crane's song of ridicule go unanswered. He started to sing:

"Ka, ka, ka, ka,
If my neck made me lose,
My feet will always let me win!
There are none quite like them
For going from lake to lake."

The crane interrupted just then with a new song:

"Listen! Listen!
Here come some cranes
And I have nothing to offer them
Neither green herbs, nor tender shoots.
I am short of everything and my boots are worn out!"

The crane tried to persuade the swan to sing and dance. The swan refused and would not budge an inch because again he would have lost: he was such a terrible dancer whereas the crane was so lightfooted.

Kajortoq and the Crow

Kajortoq, the red fox, was strolling along the edge of a cliff when she chanced to see a moose grazing on some moss. Approaching the moose Kajortoq said, "I know of a place near here where there is wild fruit. It is on a narrow ledge of rocks which we can reach by following the path halfway up the cliff."

The moose followed Kajortoq without hesitation and jumping over rock hollows, soon found himself in a precarious position on the edge of the precipice. The fox, who had moved ahead of the moose, turned and warned, "Be careful here. It is easy to lose your footing. Take care not to fall. Jump quickly to this side!" The moose did as Kajortoq directed but when his hooves landed on the slippery rocks they struck a loose stone and he fell to the bottom of the cliff. When Kajortoq reached the bottom she found the moose dead and proceeded to make a meal of her victim.

Days later she had finished all of the meat and set out to continue her hunting. Eventually she spotted a bird sitting on its eggs in a nest at the top of a tree. She called up to the bird, "I want to eat some eggs. Throw one to me!" Although the bird valued her eggs, she was frightened and allowed one of them to fall to the ground. Kajortoq ate it quickly and moved away from the tree.

Soon she was back demanding more eggs. This time the bird replied, "No, I will not give them to you." At this Kajortoq screamed, "If you don't give me some of your eggs I will take them all for I shall cut down this tree with my axe!" Intimidated, the poor bird let a few more eggs fall to the ground and the fox ate her fill and moved on.

Tulugaq, the crow, had been watching these events and now he came to speak to the bird. "Why did you let that renegade fox eat your eggs?" he asked. The bird explained that if she hadn't given Kajortoq a few of the eggs she would have used her axe to cut down the tree and all the eggs would have been lost. Tulugaq replied, "That fox is nothing but a liar; she has no axe! She is only trying to frighten you."

When the crow had gone, it was not long before Kajortoq returned demanding still more eggs and threatening once more to cut down the tree. This time the bird spoke without fear or hesitation.

"I will give you no more eggs. I am keeping them for myself."

Kajortoq was suspicious. "Who has been telling tales about me?"

"The big crow told me that you have no axe and cannot cut down this tree where I have my nest," replied the bird. "I shall give you no more eggs!"

The red fox moved off muttering, "That crow is nothing but a chatter box." She headed toward an open field where she lie down, pretending to be dead. Curious, Tulugaq approached the fox's still form, cawing noisily and pecking at her buttocks and hind feet with his beak to see if the fox would stir. With great difficulty the fox remained perfectly still until Tulugaq, certain that Kajortoq was dead, moved toward her head in order to peck out her eyes. Suddenly the crow found himself imprisoned in the fox's strong jaws.

Kajortoq carried her victim to a small hill and prepared to eat him. However before she could begin her meal, the crow spoke.

"Where is the wind coming from?" the crow asked.

The fox thought, "Are you crazy to ask such a question?"

She opened her mouth wide to say so and the crow flew away.

Lost at Sea

Nearly a hundred years ago, a group of seal hunters built their igloos at the shore of the ocean in what is known today as Stapylton Bay.

An expanse of solid ice ran from the shore well out into the sea. One day when the weather was favourable a party of men set out, as was their custom, in search of the *aglu*, the breathing holes made by the seals in the sea ice.

When they were some distance from land, the ice suddenly split between the men and the land and a vapour as thick as smoke escaped from the crevasse. Some of the hunters who were closer to the shore had time to jump to the solid ice on the other side before it was too late. However the others who were further out on the ice did not sense the danger as they were concentrating on the *aglu*, waiting for the seal to appear. It was only when one of the men, Ulukhaq, left his place in search of another *aglu* that the crevasse was noticed. Ulukhaq spotted the column of vapour and knew immediately what had happened.

The others heard him cry. "The fog is coming, the mist is rising, the ice is broken!" Calling to one another, all of the hunters ran toward the line of dark smoke which hung like a curtain between themselves and the land.

The men followed the edge of the crevasse, searching in vain for a block of ice which would take them across the water. But the thickening fog hid everything. It was not even possible to attract the attention of those who had escaped to the solid ice on the other side. After a long search, the small group of hunters met together. One of them, Kudlaluk, was missing. His companions thought that he had perhaps found safe passage to the other side and so their hopes were raised.

Just then, however, Kudlaluk reappeared. He had been unable to find a way across the crevasse. The men were forced to stay where they were and soon their ice floe was drifting into the fog where nothing could be seen. That evening the men built an igloo on the ice floe and spent the night in its shelter and warmth.

The next day their ice raft ceased drifting. The hunters found that they were west of their point of departure for they could faintly distinguish the place where their first igloos had been built on the solid ice. Their plan was to stay where they were for the entire day in order to give the newly formed ice between themselves and the mainland time to thicken. All of the men were in agreement with this except Nulialik who wanted to try and reach the shore immediately.

After some discussion, they decided to follow Nulialik. Darkness had fallen. Rather than leave the igloo through its proper entrance they made a hole in the wall large enough to crawl through. The hunters hoped to avoid the evil spirits who were watching the entrance to their igloo and who were undoubtedly responsible for their present problems. Once the passage through the wall was completed the men ran without stopping onto the ice floes, jumping here and there on the more solid chunks of ice.

Closer and closer they came to the safety of the shore. Yet with only a short distance to go the men were stopped. A large crevasse appeared before them and reluctantly the men returned to the igloo from which they had just departed. Here they remained for the better part of the winter.

During these days the men were never far from great danger. Had these been ordinary men they probably would have been lost without hope, but among them there were real *angatkut* or shamans who possessed extraordinary magical powers. Two of the shamans were Qorvik and Kudlaluk.

On one occasion, as the ice raft carrying the men was being drawn toward the west, a large ice pack bore down on top of them and threatened to crush the hunters' igloo. Qorvik used his great shamanistic powers to prevent this disaster by simply leaning against the wall of ice and thereby restraining it.

An ever present threat was the lack of the life-sustaining necessities. Hunger, thirst and the biting cold were constant companions. The snow upon which the men depended for their water supply was now saturated with salt. A burning thirst and the scarcity of food weakened the hunters to the point where their bodies were little more than skin and bones. Obviously something would have to be done if starvation and death were to be averted.

Fortunately, the shamans knew how to stop the disagreeable winds and currents. The shamans knew that the spirits who live on the ocean floor love metal objects. What could be done to please the spirits? Each hunter possessed a long-bladed, raw copper knife—a weapon which never left his side. Without it a hunter on a long journey would risk hunger if not certain death. Perhaps their fortunes would improve if they were to make a gift of the knives to the spirits.

Thus the decision was made. One after another each man sacrificed his knife. Each valued weapon was decorated with a tassel made from thin strips of skin. Then the knife was held over the surface of the water and allowed to sink to the bottom of the ocean. Still all of this was in vain and the men and their ice pack continued to drift, moving ever westward.

One knife still remained, that belonging to Qingalorqana. This knife had a beautiful raw copper blade, highly prized by its owner who was reluctant to give it up. But seeing that there was no other hope, Qingalorqana decided to follow the example set by his companions. Motioning to his friends to gather around,

he held the knife over the surface of the clear water. When it left Qingalorqana's hand the hunters were astonished to see this solid copper weapon float for a long period of time. Eventually, it disappeared from sight. Everyone took this to be a good sign; the spirits must be pleased.

Just to be certain that all would be well Qorvik performed one more magic rite. Selecting a small block of ice which the ocean had washed onto their floe, Qorvik threw it in the direction of the land. As he did so he asked the spirits to return them safely to their homes. Shortly thereafter the wind changed direction and the men knew that they were now moving toward safety.

That night the men remained in their igloo, talking among themselves and all the while waiting for the sound of the ice grinding upon the land, the sound that would signal the end of their ordeal.

The next morning land was sighted. Excitedly, the two eldest hunters cried out, "Let's go! Let's go!" One after another the men scrambled out of the igloo with Qorvik in the lead and Kudlaluk bringing up the rear.

In the faint light of the early dawn only the merest outline of the ice floe could be seen. This did not deter the men. Running and jumping from ice block to ice block the hunters made their way toward the shore. All day they worked their way through the pack ice before them. As night was beginning to close in they reached the thick ice that lined the land edge. The men were out of danger at last.

Immediately upon reaching the land the hunters stopped to quench their thirst. The pure snow that they now put into their mouths confirmed in the minds of the men that the salt-saturated snow was behind them. "There is no doubt that we have arrived. This is old, solid ice; it is land!" They shouted with joy as they ate the snow; they laughed and they cried.

They now knew where their igloos were situated and after resting they set out to be reunited with their families. Some paused along the way while others kept moving. In this manner the hunters arrived at their igloos one after another.

A storm was blowing up when they arrived. One man was outside re-covering his igloo in order to make it warm. It was he who heard the noise made by the returning hunters. As soon as he recognized the men he started to jump with joy as one would rejoice after a good hunt. Everyone emerged from their igloos and let loose a joyous howl. They had believed the men lost for good. Some of the women had even taken new husbands. But now that the hunters had returned safely everyone was overcome with happiness.

For a long time thereafter, whenever the hunters would lie down to sleep, the roll of the ocean still rocked their bodies. It became part of their souls and haunted them like a ghost.

The Wolf and the Owl

A wolf went to visit an owl. It was the time of year when the wolf shed his hair and his coat looked dirty and deplorable.

The owl made fun of his visitor: "Hey you! What a funny colour is your hair. Do you have a skin disease? You are not nice to look at. How is it that when you come to visit me you put on such old rags?"

"I assure you," replied the wolf, "I once had enough good skins from the caribou I killed to make myself some fine clothes. But when I have them I cannot keep them for long. Each spring I have a new brood of young ones and they tear the caribou skins to pieces. However if you wish, I shall find myself some new clothes. In turn, you can go and get newly dressed. Then we shall see which one of us is the more handsome! In three days my wife will have had time to sew me new ones and I shall return."

The challenge accepted, the wolf returned to his wife and children. For three days he remained in his den without bothering to prowl around the owl.

For his part, the owl spent all of his time washing his feathers and making his wife brush his black and white spots.

The three days passed and the wolf reappeared. He was handsome. His hair was long and lustrous and his chest was covered with thick hair. He had barely met the owl when he began to ridicule the bird. "Why didn't you change your clothes? What you have on your back now is no better than what you were wearing before!"

The owl had tried to make himself handsome, but he had so many feathers on his body that his efforts to beautify himself barely helped. He became angry and turned on the wolf. To avoid being bitten the wolf galloped toward his den. But the owl continued his attack, swooping down on the wolf and knocking him in the chest with the fleshy part of his breast. The force of the blows made it difficult for the wolf to continue. The owl seized him and with blows from his claws and beak soon killed the wolf.

Three days later, a female wolf with two cubs arrived at the owl's premises. She was looking for her husband. The owl watched them approach then flew away leaving behind his own young offspring. The female wolf quickly killed them. Having won revenge the wolf ran back to her den with her cubs.

The owl followed them. He attacked the cubs first. With heavy blows, he weakened and then killed each in turn. Despite the owl's repeated attacks, the female wolf ran until she dropped from exhaustion. The owl then slashed her breast to pieces, killing her as he had killed her husband.

The Deceitful Raven

It is told that in days gone by a big raven came in search of people.

Spying a settlement he swooped low over the igloos and called out, "Many visitors are on their way! It would be wise for you to go out to meet them. If you do not encounter these travellers before nightfall, make camp at the foot of the cliff."

The people in the igloos took the raven at his word and set out to meet the visitors. When night arrived they built their shelters at the foot of the cliff and soon the flames of their stone lamps were flickering brilliantly on the walls of the snow houses.

A little later, before bedtime, each lamp was put out. The raven waited until the last stone lamp was extinguished and then flew off into the darkness. He flew straight to the top of the cliff which towered over the igloos. There on the summit was an enormous overhang of snow which the slightest movement would crumble.

This raven of misfortune alighted on the snow and began to jump, run and dance about in order to cause an avalanche. His efforts were soon rewarded. The accumulated snow broke away and fell on the igloos below. The sleeping inhabitants were buried, never to awake again.

The raven waited for spring to arrive and for the snow to disappear. He waited in eager anticipation as he knew what he would find. He liked to peck out the eyes of his victims.

The snow gradually melted, exposing the bodies of the unlucky people. The raven had not waited in vain. He amused himself by emptying the eye sockets of those who had innocently followed his directions. For the entire spring he remained below the cliff, without fear of his provisions running out.

Taligvak

A long time ago, in a village on the shore of the Arctic Ocean, the seal hunters had a bad winter. Snowstorms blew constantly, making it impossible to hunt; the people went hungry.

The hunters invited well-known shamans to call upon their spirits in the big dance igloo which they called the *qalgie*. However the shamans were unable to make the seals come and famine threatened the settlement.

A young man named Taligvak lived with these people. No one liked him and he lived alone at the edge of the settlement apart from the other people. He was very poor, lacking nearly all necessities. No one wanted to give him a daughter for a wife and so Taligvak had no one to sew warm clothing for him. He did own a knife and with that he was able to build a snow house. But it was so small that he could not lie down inside it and instead had to remain in a sitting position even when trying to sleep. Moreover, as there was no stone lamp in his igloo, Taligvak suffered from the cold. When his mittens became frozen with frost he had to put them under his clothes, next to his skin, and as he slept the heat from his body would dry them.

It is possible that everyone avoided Taligvak because they were afraid of him. As young as he was, he was reputed to be a powerful shaman. It was said that he commanded strange magic forces. It was believed that there was nothing that Taligvak could not do: his aides were the spirits of the air and the darkness who, taking pity on him, would come at his call and do wonders for him. All of the people spoke in awe of the young man's strange powers but, not liking him, they had kept him at a distance. However now that they were threatened with starvation the people wondered if they should ask his help.

The people met in the *qalgie*, the big dance igloo, to discuss what they should do. They agreed that the only one who could help them in this period of ill fortune was Taligvak. Quickly, they sent three young men to bring him to the *qalgie*.

When the three men arrived at Taligvak's igloo, two of them were so afraid that they did not dare to look inside. The third man, having more courage, looked in and said, "Taligvak, the people want you to come to the *qalgie*. Come see them."

Taligvak remained silent for awhile. Finally he answered. "The wind is blowing up a storm. It is cold out and I have nothing warm to wear, not even mittens or boots. I shall not go to them."

Hearing his refusal, the messengers returned to the *qalgie*. A woman was then sent to Taligvak with a present of mittens and boots. She took him by the arm and led him back to the big igloo.

Taligvak entered the igloo by crawling through the low passageway. When he reached the entrance of the large room he refused to go inside, preferring to stand by the door, motionless, without saying a word. The people had their eyes fixed on him. One of them spoke out: "You want a warm igloo; you want to stay with us, to have good clothes, mittens and warm skins to sleep under. We shall give you all this if you will cut a hole in the ice right here at the edge of the igloo and if you will make the seals come. We are going to starve to death for certain. Catch some seals for us!"

Taligvak stayed where he was for some time. Then he went over to the wall of the *qalgie* and knelt down on the ice. "Do not watch what I do," he commanded the people. "You must begin to dance."

The people started to sing and dance while he worked at making a hole in the ice. He blew on the ice again and again and each time the magic force of his breath hollowed the surface. Eventually the ice was broken and water bubbled up into the hole.

The young man then invited the dancers to come and look. Each saw the water at the bottom of the hole with his own eyes and let out a cry of joy.

"Now," Taligvak said, "begin dancing again and do not watch what I shall do." He was holding a small magic weapon in his hand. It was a harpoon which was as small as a child's toy. He brandished it over his head and sang an invocation to the spirits that would help him:

"What joy to hear climbing from the bottom of the water

A very fat animal

Who will give to all

As much to eat as they will want!

What joy to see it stretched out

On the floor of the igloo,

When they have pulled it from

The bottom of the water!"

While singing he had harpooned a seal which had come to answer his call and he had pulled it onto the floor of the igloo. On his orders the people dragged the beast to the far side of the *qalgie* to a snow lean-to which formed a secondary room. He told them to remove the head of the harpoon from the seal's body.

When the harpoon head was brought to him he replaced it on the shaft of his weapon. He then ordered that the animal be cut up and the meat distributed.

While some ate and others sang, he again took up his vigil near the hole. He forbade the people to watch what he was doing and began to sing once more:

"What joy for the men
When on the ice
A big seal is hauled
From the hole where he came to breathe.
My harpoon line is for him
Like a snare which squeezes him!"

And again, thanks to the magic of his song, Taligvak pulled a big, fat seal onto the ice. The people cried with joy; they no longer feared that they would starve to death.

Winter passed and the darkness lifted from the sky and the earth. Spring returned and with its return the people left their camp on the ice to go inland, to hunt caribou and to fish in the lakes.

By this time, Taligvak was receiving help from the others, but he was always left somewhat alone. He also went inland, but he walked behind the others, carrying his sleeping skins, his knife and sewing implements on his back. (It was said that his sewing needles were cut from the bones of a rabbit's foot.)

The thaw soon came. Taligvak remained alone while the others camped some distance away near the Padleq River. Left by himself he saw the thaw quicken; the snow gradually disappeared from the surface of the earth, the rivers began to open up and water flowed. He saw the caribou descend toward the river. Encouraged by these signs of spring, Taligvak looked around for materials with which he could construct a kayak. He found a few pieces of wood washed up on the seashore. He placed snares in the willows and caught rabbits. He cleaned their skins and carefully extracted the hair and down.

Next, selecting those pieces of wood which were easiest to work with, he carved them with his knife into a kayak frame. This work took him some time; the sun was already becoming warmer and warmer. Taligvak saw the fish jump in the river and he caught a few of them. He saw some birds and succeeded in snaring a loon. He cut its neck in circular fashion and made some thin straps. He now had everything required to complete his kayak.

He took the rabbit skins, which he had set aside to soak in the water, and stretched them over the kayak frame. He sewed the skins together with the thin straps made from the loon. His kayak was ready.

He was in the process of trying out his kayak when a herd of caribou suddenly appeared on the opposite shore in front of him. They seemed to be ready to enter the water in order to cross the river. Taligvak prepared his kayak to chase them. His knife was his only weapon and he was frightened. Despite this, he approached one of them and killed it.

Later on, while eating his caribou meat, he looked at the shape of the bones and wondered what he could make from them. He took a shin bone, hammered it with a stone and split it lengthwise. With one half of the bone he made a sharp weapon which he mounted on a piece of wood. Now when the caribou arrived on the opposite bank of the river he was not afraid for he had in his possession a solid, pointed spear.

He set out in his kayak for the far side of the river with the intention of allowing not a single caribou to escape. In fact, through skillful use of his spear, he killed them all, one after another. None of this game was wasted. The meat and the skins were put out to dry. The marrow and tongues were preserved in bags made from the stomachs of the first animals. Nothing was thrown aside.

That same night people came to his camp. He had built himself a low-walled

shelter from stones and turf, and when he saw these people in the distance he wondered who they could be. He continued to watch them from his shelter.

As they approached he recognized them as being the people from his settlement. Quickly he rose and went to greet them. They were hungry, and hunger had driven them back to Taligvak and to the river they knew to be filled with fish at this time of year. Moreover they were curious to see if he was still alive.

Taligvak gave food to these famished people. The plate, which he placed on the ground, was an old scrap of seal skin which they had thrown away because they did not find it good enough for them. On this piece of skin Taligvak placed a little bit of meat, a small helping of marrow and a few tongues; not much of anything for a large, hungry crowd. He made the people sit on the opposite side of the plate from him, told them not to watch what he was going to do, and began to sing:

"They have arrived at Taligvak's
And it is lucky that I have some tongues to offer them
And that I killed a very fat caribou
That, you know all about!
No need to tell you.
But look at this plate,
This poor plate of nothing.
It is full to overflowing. . .
It is overflowing!"

And the people saw the plate in which Taligvak had put so very little fill itself more and more. Taligvak continued his magic chant:

"From the banks of the Padleq River,
They came to my place

And I killed a very fat caribou
With my kayak sewn with thin straps
That, you know all about!
No need to tell you.
But look at this plate,
This poor plate of nothing,
It is full to overflowing. . .
It is overflowing!"

The meat continued to grow on the plate made from skin. Many people were there and they were very hungry. They had not eaten meat for a long time. They ate until they were gorged, but they were not able to finish the contents of poor Taligvak's magic plate.

The Hunter and the Children

One day an old man went seal hunting a short distance from the land. Close to his chosen hunting spot the sea coast formed an abrupt rocky spur on the top of which lay a high bank of snow. Below this cliff some children were laughing and shouting while playing their games.

Thinking only of the seal that he hoped to kill, the hunter positioned himself beside a likely breathing hole. Here he waited, motionless. Eventually the sound of the seal's breathing was heard. Quietly he raised his harpoon, ready for the fatal strike. Suddenly the silence was broken! The noise of the children playing at the foot of the cliff distracted the old man and warned the seal. Diving into the deep water, the seal escaped.

The old man lowered his harpoon in a bad mood and declared, "Those children! I hope the cliff of snow falls and buries them!" However nothing happened and the children continued their loud games.

Once more the hunter resumed his vigil at the breathing hole. Again the seal returned. Raising his arm with the harpoon extended the hunter waited. For a second time he could not strike. The laughter of the children so upset the old man that the seal got away unharmed.

At this turn of events the old hunter impatiently called upon his shamanistic powers. He called forth the spirits which brought bad luck: "Let those children be buried under the snow!"

And it happened.

An avalanche of snow fell from the top of the cliff and swallowed the children. As the story goes their cries were heard for a long time, gradually growing weaker until at last all were silent.

When the parents of the children realized what had happened they sought revenge and went to find the old man. Seeing them come the hunter tried to flee. Just as he was about to be caught he called upon his shamanistic powers one last time and lifted himself into the air. His pursuers watched him go up into the sky, finally disappearing and then reappearing as a shooting star. On a clear night, if you look carefully, you can still see the old man fleeing through the heavens.

Kidnapped by Wolves

It was summer on the riverside in the high land. There a married couple had built a rudimentary shelter with walls made of turf and a roof of caribou skin. They slept when the sun was at its lowest point on the horizon. During the day they went fishing, watching the fish swim through the meanders of their stone weir which was built in the river. Harpooning the fish, the husband and wife would cut them up and place the fillets in the sun to dry.

One day they had left their sleeping child in the shelter while they worked at enlarging the fish drying area a short distance from their home. They had made scarecrows all around their provisions of fish. Piles of stones were used for the bodies and lumps of turf were placed atop these piles to resemble heads. In this manner their food was protected from marauding gulls and crows.

The man and woman were engaged in constructing more scarecrows when a male wolf came up to them. He had taken off his skin and left it behind some rocks. He looked like a man. The only difference in his appearance was that he had the feet of a wolf, but the couple did not notice this.

The wolf walked over and invited them to take off their work clothes. "Dance," he told them. "I shall sing for you."

This being, half man and half wolf, had a plan in mind. He and his wife had observed the couple with their child. They wanted to steal the little boy. The female wolf, who was hiding not far away, was awaiting a chance to snatch the child. While the couple were dancing she would take the sleeping infant from the shelter and run away with him.

The man and the woman liked dancing and accepted the wolf's invitation. They took off their clothing and began dancing to the rhythm of their visitor's songs. Unknown to them the wolf was singing magic chants and the couple was soon under his spell. Their minds floated into another world; they had forgotten everything, even their child.

When the female wolf saw them in this trance-like state she took the child and fled to her den. As soon as he thought that his wife had made it safely home with the stolen child, the wolf stopped the dance and left the couple. Putting on his skin he once more became a real wolf. The man and the woman came to their senses, saw the escaping wolf, and immediately went to their shelter to check on their child.

The infant had disappeared, apparently without a single trace. His parents searched the entire area but found nothing. They had returned to their shelter when, in the entrance way, they noticed several pieces of wolf hair. This clue made them think that it was a companion of their visitor who had stolen the child.

They had a dog and the next day they made him search for the wolf's tracks. They walked for a long time without success. The ground was very dry and revealed few tracks at all. Just before giving up completely they found the wolves' den. They tied their dog out of sight and hiding themselves, they began to watch the comings and goings of the wolves. They observed them without their skins, acting like real human beings. The female was holding the child in her arms, rocking him to sleep on her knee.

Speaking quietly so as not to reveal their presence, the wife said, "If we had two bows, we could shoot arrows at them and kill both of them at once while they are asleep. Let's go home and you can make me a bow."

The husband found his wife's suggestion to be a good one, so they returned home. Back in their shelter, the man made his wife a bow and an abundant supply of arrows for her as well as for himself. He cut the arrowheads from antlers and sharpened their points. To kill the wolf-men they would use arrows which had never been used for other hunting.

They returned to the wolves' den and decided to wait until they were sound asleep to take them by surprise. At this time the male and female were feeding the child what appeared to be caribou fat. When the meal was over they put the child to bed between the two of them. Soon they were asleep. They suspected nothing.

Emerging from their hiding place, the child's parents let fly their arrows and both wolves were killed instantly. But the she-wolf had been holding the little boy tightly against her body. The arrow that pierced her chest killed the child at the same moment.

The Legend of the Coppermine River

A long time ago a young girl named Itiktajjak left her home to go in search of some firewood. While she was walking along, a brown bear picked up her scent and began to follow her. Realizing that the bear was on her track, the young girl immediately fell to the ground, stiffened her muscles and pretended to be dead. The bear came upon his prey but thought that the young girl had frozen solid. Without hesitation he heaved her upon his back and started to carry her to his cave where his family was waiting.

It happened that the path taken by the bear led through tall willow bushes. Thinking that she might hinder the bear's progress, Itiktajjak hooked her stiffened arms around the branches and forced the bear to slow his pace. The bear struggled and fought to free his burden from the bushes but the harder he tried the more tired he became.

He arrived at his cave to find his two devilish cubs playing on the large platform that served as their bed. Mother bear was asleep. Father bear was exhausted by his difficult journey and lay the girl on the floor saying to his cubs, "Here is something for you to eat."

On hearing these words the cubs performed a joyful dance around Itiktajjak who still appeared to be quite frozen. Father bear wanted to rest. His children wanted to play. In exasperation the old bear motioned the cubs to be quiet. "Later on you will have some of the girl to eat," he told them.

Hearing the excitement the mother bear awoke, climbed out of bed and with

an axe in her hand went to examine this piece of game lying on the floor. Finding the girl to be very stiff she laid the axe on the floor near Itiktajjak and went back to bed.

When Itiktajjak sensed that both mother and father had gone to sleep, she opened her eyes for the first time. The two cubs, ever watchful of the young girl's movements, cried, "Father! She has thawed! She opened her eyes!"

But the old bear would not be disturbed and growled, "Let her open her eyes, but let me be! She has tired me out already by gripping the willow branches." The bear quickly fell into a deep sleep.

Itiktajjak continued to pretend to be dead. She had noticed the axe lying close by, but before she opened her eyes once more she wanted to be certain that all of the bears were asleep. Very soon thereafter all was quiet in the cave. The cubs, tired from their play, had fallen asleep.

Sensing that it was safe to open her eyes, the young girl quickly got up, grabbed the axe and hit the mother bear a blow on the ear. Immediately the cave was filled with the old bear's cries of pain. Itiktajjak glanced quickly about her and saw that the father bear was awakening. She fled from the cave, pursued by the male bear who was now fully aroused.

Knowing only that she must run as quickly as she could, Itiktajjak ran until she came to a small stream. She jumped across, then paused briefly on the other side. She took her little finger and with it traced a line through the water. While so doing she repeated the magic words, "river, river, make your path cross here." The words were barely uttered when the stream swelled to a torrent of water, separating Itiktajjak from the old bear.

"What can I do now?" thought the bear. "There isn't any way for me to get across this raging river." With these thoughts the bear paced up and down the bank on his side of the river. Finally he called out to the girl, "How did you manage to cross this river?"

Without a moment's hesitation Itiktajjak replied, "I put my nose in it and drank until the water disappeared and a dry path appeared."

The father bear thought that he could do the same so he began to lap up the water as quickly as he could. He drank and drank and the more he swallowed the fatter he became. Finally, with one last swallow, he exploded and the water from his body spread a heavy mist over everything.

Itiktajjak watched all of this happening and noticed that clouds were beginning to form from the mist. Never before had clouds been seen in this area. From these clouds water was soon to fall into the river which had been created when the young girl drew her finger through the waters. This river has come to be known as the *Qorlorloq* or Coppermine, the river whose course is scattered with waterfalls.

The Ghost Hunter

A young boy lived alone with his grandmother. As he grew older he became obsessed with a fear of ghosts. Such was his distress that he could not sleep at nights.

Repeatedly his grandmother told him, "Go to sleep like everyone else. There is no point in worrying, anyway; if you ever see a ghost you can be certain that it will quickly overpower you."

The boy, being stubborn by nature, would invariably reply, "No, no ghost would ever do that to me!"

When he became a young man, the boy decided to build himself an igloo. However he chose to place his home in an area somewhat apart from the other igloos so that he would be able to see anything that might approach from any direction.

His igloo was built like a large fort. Windows were cut out all around the sides and openings were made from which arrows could be shot at any evil spirits that might appear.

Once the igloo was completed the young man took up a nightly watch from within his fortress. Equipped with the bow and arrows given to him by his grandmother, he waited for the ghosts to appear. His grandmother and some of the other older people tried to persuade the young man to go to bed at night. They were afraid of what might happen to him if a ghost did appear.

"You will be killed!" they warned.

Obstinately the young man would reply, "No, no, nothing can happen to me." He was wrong to ignore the wisdom of his elders but obsessed as he was with his ideas, no one could change his mind.

Late one night, while maintaining his usual vigil, he thought he saw something move outside his window. He watched carefully, hoping that at last he might see a ghost. He strained to see what it could be. To his surprise it was not a ghost, but a beautiful young woman dressed in fine furs. She was standing near his grandmother's dwelling.

The young man was fascinated by her beauty and the more he watched the more smitten he became with her loveliness. He wanted her for his wife. Overcome with emotion, the young man forgot about everything else, including ghosts and spirits, bows and arrows. Without thinking any further and without even dressing in warm clothing, he dashed from his igloo and ran towards her.

Seeing the young man approach the woman spoke, "Come with me and you will be my husband. Let us go to my parents' home. Look over there and you can see the light from our igloo. It is the window of my father's house."

The young man looked and saw the illuminated window. After taking a few steps he hesitated, "No, I will not follow you. I am going to remain here."

The girl insisted, "But it is so near. Come, and we shall live together as husband and wife."

The girl's beauty and persistence finally overcame the boy's reluctance. He followed her through the night toward the bright light of her father's igloo.

For a long time they walked on together. Periodically the boy would turn around to view the receding lights of his settlement. It seemed as if they were getting farther and farther away from his home but the girl's home was no closer to them.

The boy was beginning to tire from the long journey. By now his own settlement had disappeared from view and only the encouragement of the girl kept him going. It was a great relief when they finally arrived at the girl's home. Inside the igloo they were welcomed by the parents and the girl's two younger brothers.

Seeing these people together it now dawned on the young man what had happened. These were not people at all. They were ghosts. He, who had always wanted to see a ghost, had been tricked by what he thought was a beautiful girl. But there was no turning back. The young man and the girl became man and wife.

For a long time the two of them lived together. Eventually the young man became unhappy at the lack of interesting and exciting things to do. His brothers-in-law went out on hunting expeditions but having no kayak or weapons, he remained at home. When the hunters returned with an abundance of game, the young man became jealous. He found it difficult to repress his feelings. He went to his wife and told her how much he would like to go hunting.

"Perhaps your father, who does not hunt, could lend me his bow?"

The girl went to her father. "My husband would like to borrow your bow so that he can go hunting with my brothers."

The old man had no objections and so the husband made plans to leave for the caribou grounds. Just prior to his departure the old man offered him some advice. "Do not become separated from your brothers-in-law for any reason. If you see a caribou grazing on the side of the mountain be careful not to pursue him!"

The young man followed this advice and made repeated hunting trips. Each time he would return to the settlement with a large supply of game. But one day, while he was travelling along with his two companions, the young man said: "I saw something over there on the side of the mountain. It must be a caribou."

The brothers-in-law replied, "No, we cannot hunt that one. That is the caribou that our father forbids us to kill. We shall leave that one alone. There are plenty of others." With that the two brothers went hunting elsewhere.

The young man was unable to dismiss the thought of the lone caribou from his mind. "Why does the old man not want us to go after that one?" he wondered. For some days thereafter the young man was haunted by thoughts of the caribou on the side of the mountain.

One day, while on another hunting trip, he made the decision to go after this caribou. The brothers-in-law tried to dissuade him but the young man became stubborn. He left his companions and set out on his own. He would kill the caribou, this caribou that was so mysteriously protected.

Approaching the mountain with caution, the hunter stalked his victim. He moved in as close as he could and then with deadly aim, let fly his arrow. The caribou fell. Immediately the young man started to skin the animal.

No sooner had the skinning commenced than a fog began to close in around him. Working quickly the hunter tried to finish his task before the fog completely blotted out the trail back to the settlement. When he had finished he left the caribou carcass on the ground, covered it with the stomach contents so that no animals would touch it, looked about him to be sure of his directions and set out for home.

Try as he might he could not find the right path. Each time he managed to proceed only a short distance before being confronted by a sharp cliff. He would then retrace his steps to the carcass, head himself in another direction and set out once more. The cliff rose from the fog to bar his path again and

again. Moreover it seemed that the wall of rocks was closing in on him. He would be crushed!

Fortunately the young man always carried a charm of considerable magic with him. It was a piece of clothing with very short sleeves and was made from the skin of his ancestors. This garment was worn next to his body. Realizing the great danger he was in, the young man now called on the magic powers of his charm. He seized a sleeve and half removing the garment cried out to his ancestor, "Grandmother, I am in great danger!"

With this one call, the weather suddenly improved. The fog lifted and the stranded hunter was able to return home.

His in-laws had been worried about him. They wanted to know what had happened. At first the young man was reluctant to say anything. However his in-laws were insistent and after much persuasion he told them of the caribou, the fog and of his plea to his grandmother for help. But he did not tell them about the magic garment. The in-laws were not pleased. They forbade the young man from going on further hunting trips. He would have to remain at home while the brothers did the hunting.

For a long time the young hunter was left alone with little to do. He could only watch enviously while his brothers-in-law went in search of more game. As before, his feelings of jealousy finally got the better of him.

He spoke to his wife: "Your father has a kayak and a harpoon. I could make good use of these and follow the others when they go seal hunting."

His wife agreed to ask her father. "My husband wishes to hunt the seals. Could he borrow your kayak and harpoon?"

The father had no objections. "You may use them," he told the son-in-law. "My kayak is on the river bank and my harpoon is inside it. However before you go hunting there is something that you should know. You must only hunt the seals on this side of the island. Do not go to the other side. The seals on the far side are vicious. In your travels be sure to stay on the side closest to the land."

The three young hunters took the old man's advice and hunted the seals together, remembering not to go on the far side of the island. For many days they continued to hunt in this fashion.

Then one day it occurred to the husband that he should go to the other side of the island. He mentioned this idea to his brothers-in-law, but they would have none of it.

"No, we shall not go there; our father has forbidden it," they replied.

The young man was not so easily convinced. He would go by himself. Leaving his companions, he paddled toward the forbidden area. When he had reached the far side and was about to explore the shoreline, an extraordinary beast suddenly emerged from the depths of the sea and swam toward the hunter's kayak.

The young man threw his harpoon. The weapon found its mark and at the same instant the young man lost consciousness.

When he awoke he did not know where he was. He found himself on an ice field from which no land was visible. Looking around him the hunter spotted a huge snow house as large as a dance igloo. A man stood outside and motioned to him to enter.

The young man went inside. Around the igloo, standing in a circle, was a crowd of people. Lying on the floor was the monstrous seal that he had harpooned. The people pressed around him.

"You have killed our friend," they said. "Remove your harpoon from his body. When you have done so, cut yourself a large piece of meat. You will need this for food on the long journey that awaits you." The young man followed their instructions and made ready for a lengthy trip.

Dragging his kayak overland, the young hunter travelled throughout the long winter months. In time the kayak became worn to the point where it had to be dismantled. From the remaining pieces a package was made which the young man carried on his back.

By springtime this seemingly endless journey was far from over. With the arrival of the warmer weather other problems had to be faced. Pools of water were lying everywhere. Even when he reached land this problem remained. The island upon which the hunter was walking became covered with water. Moreover the depth of the water was increasing constantly. Recognizing that he was in extreme danger, the young man seized the sleeve of his magic garment and cried out, "Grandmother, I am in great danger!"

Immediately a great transformation took place. The young man was lifted into the air and was changed into a sea swallow. In bird-like fashion he was able to continue his journey, diving down over the water to snatch scorpion fish whenever he was hungry.

Eventually his flight took him to the area where he had lived with his grandmother long ago. Now everything was in ruins. All of the people were gone. His only hope was to return to his in-laws and so he used the magic power of the short-sleeved garment to transform himself back to a man.

Arriving at his in-laws' igloo the young man was confronted by his relatives. They were very curious about his strange disappearance and had many questions to ask. At first he refused to answer. He was ashamed to admit that he had gone to the far side of the island. But his in-laws would not leave him alone. In exasperation he finally gave in and decided to talk.

"All right! I am going to tell you everything, but first bring me a small bowl of water and place it at my feet."

Seated on the edge of the bed with the bowl of water before him on the floor, the young man proceeded to recount the entire story. No details were omitted save one. He did not mention his magic garment made from the skin of his ancestors. It was his last protection.

The young man completed his story by confessing that he had wanted to return to his grandmother's igloo, but that upon finding it deserted and in ruins, he had had no choice but to come back to the home of his in-laws.

His story angered the family but no sooner was the narrative completed than the young man, his magic garment in his hand, leaped from the bed and threw himself headfirst into the bowl of water. He disappeared and was gone forevermore.

The Blind Boy and the Loon

A woman lived with her son and daughter in a far away land. The son, although young in years, was already a skillful hunter and the four storage platforms built around the igloo were always filled with meat. His success at hunting was so great that the family never wanted for anything.

The young hunter's sister loved him dearly but his mother gradually grew tired of his hunting activities. Each time her son returned home with some game she would have to work hard at cleaning and skinning the animals and in preparing the meat for storage. As time went on the woman wished more and more to be able to rest but as long as her son continued to hunt this was not possible. Eventually her weariness turned to hatred.

One day, while her son was sleeping, the woman took a piece of dirty blubber and rubbed it on his eyes, wishing as she did so that he would become blind. When the young man awoke his eyesight was gone. Try as he might he could see nothing but a dim whiteness.

From that day on increasing misery became the lot of the family. The son could do nothing but sit on his bed. His mother tried to provide food for the family by trapping foxes and hunting ptarmigan and ground squirrels. Yet when food was available the woman refused to give her son anything to eat or drink but the worst parts of the meat and some foul drinking water brought from the lake. Throughout the spring and summer the three people lived in this manner.

One day shortly after the arrival of winter, the young hunter heard steps on the snow. It was a polar bear trying to get into the igloo through the thin ice-window. Asking for his bow, he told his mother to aim the arrow while he pulled back the string. When all was in readiness the son let fly the arrow. Hearing the sound of the arrow as it thudded into the flesh of the bear, the son was confident that the kill had been made.

"I got him!" he cried.

"No," retorted his mother, "you merely struck an old piece of hide."

Shortly thereafter the smell of bear meat boiling in the cooking pot filled the igloo. The son said nothing but kept wondering why his mother had lied to him.

When the meat was cooked the woman fed her daughter and herself. To her son, she gave some old fox meat. It was only when she had left the igloo to get water from the lake that the young hunter was brought some bear meat by his sister.

Four long years went by while the son remained blind. Then one night, as the fluttering of wings and the cries of the birds announced the coming of spring, the son heard the call of the red-throated loon. As had been his habit during his blindness he began to crawl on his hands and knees to the lake where he knew the loon would be found.

When he arrived at the water's edge the bird came close to him and said, "Your mother made you blind by rubbing dirt into your eyes while you slept. If you wish, I can wash your eyes for you. Lie flat on my back and hold me by my neck. I shall carry you."

The son doubted that such a small bird would be able to perform such a feat, but the loon reassured him.

"Don't think those thoughts. Climb onto my back. I am going to dive with you

into deep water. When you begin to lose your breath shake your body to signal me."

The young man did as he was told and down into the lake dove the loon with the hunter on his back. As they descended into the water the son could feel the body of the loon growing larger and larger and between his hands the neck seemed to be swelling. When he could hold his breath no longer he shook his body as he had been instructed and the loon brought him up to the surface.

"What can you see?" the loon asked.

"I can see nothing but a great light," replied the son.

"I shall take you down into the water once more," said the loon. "When you begin to choke, shake your body a little."

This time the dive lasted a long time but when they finally surfaced the young man could see clearly. He could distinguish the smallest rocks on the mountains far away. He described what he could see to the loon.

"My blindness is gone! My sight is sharper than before!"

"Your eyesight is too sharp for your own good," the loon told him. "Come down with me once more and your sight will be restored as it was before your blindness."

And it was so. When the young man came out of the water for the last time his eyesight was as it had been. Now the hunter could see the loon clearly and he realized that the bird was as large as a kayak.

When they had reached the lake shore the son asked the loon what he could give to him in return for his kindness.

The loon replied, "I do not want anything for myself other than a few fishes. Put some in the lake for me once in a while. This is the only food that I look for."

The son agreed and proceeded to return to his home. He was painfully surprised to see the wretched conditions in which he had been forced to live while he was blind. The skins he had used to sleep in were filthy with dirt and bugs. His drinking water and food were crawling with lice. Nevertheless he sat down in the corner and waited for his mother to awaken.

When his mother awoke the young hunter asked for food and drink. "I am hungry and thirsty. First bring me something to drink."

His mother did as she was told but the water she brought was so dirty that her son handed the cup back to her saying, "I will not touch such filth!"

"So you can see, my son," said the woman. She went then to fetch some clean food and water.

In time the young hunter was his old self again and was able to resume his successful hunting trips as before. A year went by during which time the storage platforms were once more filled with an abundance of game.

The following spring the hunter made ready to go whale hunting. He put a new skin cover on his whale boat, made lines, harpoons and spears. When the sea was free of ice he launched his boat and took his mother with him in search of whales.

"Mind the helm," he told her. "I shall look after the harpooning."

Here and there they saw a few whales blowing but the young hunter was waiting until they found a big one close to their boat. Eventually he called out to his mother who, not knowing what her son was about to do, came to assist him. He threw his harpoon, making certain that its head had caught in the flesh of the whale and then quickly tied the other end of the line to his mother's wrist and threw her overboard.

Caught as she was the woman was dragged through the water, bobbing up and down in the waves. She cried out and reproached her son saying, "When

you were young I gave you my breast to suckle. I fed you and kept you clean. And now you do this to me!"

Finally she disappeared from sight. For years to come hunters claimed that they saw her in the waves and heard her song of despair as it was carried far and wide by the winds.

The Huntress

A long time ago in the village of Tikeraq there lived a man and his wife. They had a daughter who was a great huntress and whose endurance and strength were exceptional. When she went on hunting trips by kayak she would travel far away and leave the other hunters behind. Often she would wait until the other hunters had disappeared from her view before she would set out. Then, rowing quickly, she would catch up to them in a very short time.

She used a long, two-seated kayak. Her father was happy to steer while she rowed and threw the harpoon. One day father and daughter left home in their kayak. They hunted for some time and then decided to return home. On their way back, a beast appeared from the sea and came toward them, snarling furiously. When the beast neared the kayak, the girl threw her harpoon. In the same instant she fell into a faint.

When she regained consciousness and opened her eyes she found herself kneeling on an unknown shore. She looked all around, not knowing where to go. At last she set out in a westerly direction, following the coastline. She stopped several times to look for signs that would reveal the presence of people, but there was nothing, not even the faintest signs of habitation.

After a long walk she came upon some wood cuttings. From that point onward she frequently found other pieces of wood and they appeared to be increasingly fresher. She knew that soon she would encounter people.

A little further on she came upon a kayak which had been left on the shore.

She was glancing about for its owner when a voice said, "My kayak has trapped someone. If it is a man, I shall kill him. If it is a woman, she will live." No sooner had the girl heard these words than the owner of the kayak came running up to her. Taking her by the arm, the man led her to his igloo and made her his wife.

This man often went hunting, rising very early in the morning and travelling long hours in his kayak. He was a shaman who could take this marvelous kayak over land as well as water. When he was away hunting his wife remained in the igloo occupying her time with various household tasks.

Each time she was left alone like this, a poor boy came to visit her. She never saw him approach, nor was she able to determine where he came from. One moment he wasn't there; in the next instant he was standing beside her. When the young woman noticed his presence and had finished her work, she always gave the boy a small piece of meat. Taking the food the boy would then disappear as quietly as he had come. By watching him leave one day the young woman was able to discover his home. The poor boy lived in his grandmother's igloo which was in fact close by, but which was so hidden from view that the young woman had not noticed it.

One morning, when her work was done and she had given the little orphan some food, he spoke: "Grandmother wants you to come."

Immediately the girl followed him to the old woman's igloo. As soon as she saw her, the grandmother began talking.

"You have made my grandson's life happy by giving him something to eat. He is grateful to you. This is why I want to warn you that a great danger awaits you. This man whom you have taken as your husband is tired of you. Soon he is going to kill you. He has already had many wives and when he be-

came weary of them he killed them. When he returns from his trip it will be your turn. His storehouse is filled with the flesh of his dead wives.

"Alone you have no chance to escape him. He will kill you too. Those other women never valued my grandson. They never gave him any food. That is why I never did anything for them. But I want to help you. You will come back here tomorrow. It will not be easy for me to save you from this danger, but I will try. Now hurry home before your husband comes back!"

The woman returned home. When her husband came in from hunting she noticed that he had changed. He was irritable; he did not even glance at her. It was as if he were completely disgusted with her. The fact that he refused to look her in the face confirmed her suspicions and convinced her that what the old woman had said was true. The next morning, when her husband had departed and as soon as her housework was done, she went to the old woman's igloo.

The grandmother immediately announced: "He will try to kill you when he returns at dusk. I haven't much which will protect you from him. All I have is a small pail. I know of nothing else that can save you from this danger."

The old woman continued to speak in vivid terms as if she could visualize the scene she described. "Here is your husband who is preparing to return to his igloo to kill you. When he arrives, remain here. He is on his way now. Take this pail which is made from seal skin and which has something in the bottom of it."

The movements and the words of the grandmother were those of a shaman. One would have sworn that she was beside the man and was imitating everything he did. "He is at his igloo. He enters. He looks for you. He thinks you have disappeared. He goes outside. He looks for you around the igloo. He gets into his magic kayak. He comes here. Take this pail in your hand!"

Saying this, the shaman gave the magic bucket to the girl. "Look outside; when the bow of the kayak appears throw the pail on top of it. Here he comes! In a moment he will appear in the entrance way. There he is!"

The bow of the marvelous kayak was barely in the entrance when the girl threw the bucket on it. Immediately she lost consciousness and no longer knew what was going on around her.

When she revived, she found herself once again kneeling on a strange shore, not knowing where to go. She set out to walk along the edge of the sea. From time to time she stopped to rest. Eventually she came to an igloo and entered.

Inside, all alone, was a woman. The woman did not offer her visitor any food. Rather, she excused herself by saying, "I am not offering you anything to eat because I am afraid of what my older brother will say."

The young woman from Tikeraq remained but a short time. When she was ready to go the woman of the igloo offered this advice: "Do not look back when you depart. Only when you have gone some distance can you turn your head if you wish."

The girl followed these directions. After walking for some time she looked back and saw a huge wild animal, the like of which she had not seen before, lying on the ground beside the igloo.

Walking on, she saw in the distance another igloo. Several people lived there and here they gave her food and let her sleep. The next morning after another meal, one of the men questioned her: "Are you going to stay with us?"

"No," she replied, "I am going on."

"In that case, where are you going?"

"That way toward the west; that is the direction in which I am going."

The man then told her: "In that place where you want to go there are beings which kill men. They are not far from here. You, being a woman, will be killed without hesitation. Just recently our child was murdered. You have no weapon with which to defend yourself. Here, take this. With this you will be able to get away from them."

The man took a short-handled knife from his belt. The handle was so short that it could only be held with difficulty. However its small size made the knife easy to conceal in a pocket or a belt. It was a magic weapon which had the power to kill terrible things. "Here," declared the man, "is a weapon which will save you from danger."

To teach the young woman how to use it, the man moistened the blade with spittle and lodged its handle in the igloo wall beside him. Despite herself the girl now found herself being drawn irresistibly toward the sharp copper blade. Try as she might she could not stop herself from being drawn to the blade. Having demonstrated its powers, the man took the knife and gave it to her saying, "Here, take this and carry it with you."

Taking her leave the girl walked on until she arrived at the igloos of the beasts she had been warned of. She was met by the servant of one of the ogres who led her by the arm to the igloo of his master.

Seeing the girl the ogre spoke: "A woman! This is one who doesn't have much longer to live."

After a short silence the girl replied: "Yes, I am but a woman. I do not have much longer to live."

The ogre spoke again: "This is a woman with a glib tongue. She doesn't have much longer to live."

Once more the girl replied: "Yes, I have a glib tongue and I don't have much longer to live."

At this point the ogre prepared to jump at the girl. She cried out: "Look, I am but a woman and I have not much longer to live." With that, she pulled the knife from her belt, wet the blade with spittle and stuck the handle in the snow on her side of the igloo. The magic of the knife drew the ogre toward the blade. He stamped his feet and tried to resist but his efforts were wasted. Faster and faster he was drawn to the knife. Despite himself he was thrown upon the weapon. The wound was fatal.

When the news of the ogre's death was known, the village people came to thank the girl for ridding them of this menace. Thinking that more man-killers might be in the area the girl asked: "Where must I go now to find more like him?"

"Here, there are no more," replied the people, "and we are very happy because we have been so afraid. Over there at Tikeraq, however, there is an ogre who kills travellers. We have heard this from people who live on the land and who go there to get seal oil."

This news made the girl think back over the past. She wondered how this could be in her own village of Tikeraq which had never been plagued by such beasts. "The reports must be true. I remember that in days gone by the land people came to our settlement, to Tikeraq, to get their oil." Thinking these thoughts, she resumed her journey.

When she arrived in sight of the igloos of Tikeraq she was met by another ogre's servant who took her to his master's home. Entering the igloo the girl was immediately recognized by those present. Her father, more than the others, was full of joy.

"Since you disappeared, I have done nothing but kill people. I myself have become a man-killer. From now on, that is finished. I shall kill no one else."

The daughter then repeated the adventures that had befallen her since the day she had fainted in her father's kayak. When she had finished her story, her father explained what had happened to him and his people.

"We were the only ones who ate the meat of the terrible beast that you harpooned that day. There is still some left. We gave no one else any of it. Perhaps it was the meat that made me into an ogre. But with you gone we had no one to hunt for us. I killed those who came here for meat."

The young woman took out her knife, moistened it and put it beside her. Her father and the other people in the igloo were drawn to it and would have been stabbed had not the girl removed it in time. "It was this blade that saved me," she said. "I used it to kill the ogre."

The father was frightened by this demonstration but he was happier to have his daughter back. He declared he would never kill again.

The Eagle and the Hunter

There was once a man who never killed anything simply for the pleasure of killing. He would never have done needless harm to the smallest of beasts, not even to a spider. However one day, when an eagle landed near him, he took his bow and killed it with an arrow. Taking the bird to his lodging, he skinned it without damaging its feathers, without losing a single wisp of its down. He dried the eagle and hung it on his igloo wall. The meat he ate without wasting a bite. The few remaining bones he burned.

A while later, as he was leaving his igloo, he saw two more eagles alight nearby. As he prepared to shoot them, they removed their headpieces to reveal men's faces.

One of them spoke. "Our mother has sent us to get you. My brother and I are going to take you to her. We shall take turns carrying you. When one of us wants to rest his wings, the other will carry you. After our mother has finished telling you what she has to say, we shall bring you back here."

The man followed them without hesitation. He lay down and curled up and one of the eagles enveloped him in its long tail feathers. In this fashion the eagles flew away with the man, passing him from one to the other during the journey. While being carried in this manner, the man heard a persistent noise. It was a regular beating sound which did not stop but grew louder and louder.

Their destination lay in a strange country. When they had arrived, the eagles set the man down in front of an igloo. Inside was an eagle-woman who greeted them with a smile. It was the mother. Her heartbeat was very loud. This was the sound that the man had heard from far away.

The woman spoke to the visitor. "I thank you for what you did for my son. You wasted neither his meat nor his feathers. You kept his plumage intact, dried it and placed it in the warmth of your igloo. I thank you again and I would like to do something for you. Look, and take whatever pleases you."

The eagle-woman proceeded to show the man all of the treasures over which she was guardian. There were all kinds of things. All of the animals in the world were arranged on shelves. The man looked but he hesitated to take anything as he was afraid of the woman whose son he had killed. The woman insisted. "Choose whatever you wish and my sons will carry whatever you want back to your home."

When the woman showed him the white foxes, the man saw that there were many of them and so he accepted her offer. The woman then took some of the foxes and cut off small pieces of their ears which she put into a bag made from a transparent membrane. The woman gave the bag to the man and told her sons to take him back home.

Just before he left, the eagle-woman gave him some advice. "My children will take you close to your own country, but you will still have a short distance to go to reach your igloo. If you become thirsty while walking home, take great care to keep your eyes closed when you bend down to drink the water."

The two brothers flew off with the man and returned him to his country. They put him down in a place where he was within easy walking distance of his home. As soon as they had left, the man set out for his igloo, the membrane package strapped to his shoulders. As he walked, the man became tired and thirsty. All this time he had been thinking over the eagle-woman's advice, but when he stopped to drink, he completely forgot about it. He bent low over the water with his eyes open!

In the water's reflection he saw the package on his back inflate, become huge and then burst. The tiny pieces of ears came to life, changing to real white foxes which tumbled out on the ground and ran away.

The man continued on to his igloo with very few foxes left in his sack. It was only with the help of his neighbours that he was able to catch a few of those that had escaped.

The Lazy Son-in-law

A married couple had an only daughter who would not marry. It was not because her father had not tried to find a son-in-law. He had travelled near and far in quest of a partner for her, but all the available boys he had approached declined his offer. They didn't want her, it was said, because her hair was stiff and thick like the nerves of a caribou leg.

This was the situation when one day visitors arrived at their camp. The son of these strangers had no wife and the father of the forsaken girl saw in him a potential son-in-law. So strong was the father's insistence that this young man consented to marry his daughter and remained in the camp while his parents continued on their travels.

The girl with the stiff hair had finally found a husband. However if the father thought he had made a good choice in selecting a son-in-law, he was soon to be disappointed. The poor boy had no weapons, no equipment, and was good for practically nothing. A bow, some arrows, a knife to work wood and bone, a hunting knife—indeed everything that a hunter needs had to be provided by his father-in-law. His mother-in-law made him some suits and boots.

Once outfitted, however, the young man never went hunting. He stayed in the igloo, satisfied to do nothing and with no intention of ever leaving.

The father-in-law was patient and waited for the boy to decide to go hunting. Days passed and still the boy gave no sign of any interest. Finally, the father-in-law could restrain himself no longer and asked, "When will my son-in-law bring us some caribou to eat?" At these words of reproach the son-in-law jumped with surprise.

"If you want caribou, there are some over there at the foot of the cliff," he replied.

"Well, go there," said the father-in-law, "use your arrows, and when you return I shall make you some new ones. Go after the caribou!"

The young man left for the hunt. He was gone three days and when he returned it was obvious that he had failed completely. Not only did he not kill a single caribou, but all of his arrows were broken and the soles of his boots were worn out.

His mother-in-law put new soles on his boots. His father-in-law repaired the arrows and made some new ones. When everything was ready they hoped to see him go out again but they waited in vain. Once more the father-in-law decided to speak.

"When will my son-in-law bring us some hare?"

"If someone wants to eat hare," replied the young man, "there are some quite near here. They can be seen in the willows where the water has cut streams in the hillside."

The son-in-law left at once. In three days he returned, but with empty hands: no hare! The soles of his boots were full of holes and his arrows were in pieces. His father-in-law worked for a long time to repair the broken arrows and to make new ones. Likewise his mother-in-law repaired his boots. Eventually everything was ready once more and the parents hoped that the young man would resume hunting and bring home some game. However the son-in-law showed no more interest in going out after game on this occasion than he had previously.

The father was forced to speak yet again: "When will my son-in-law give us some ptarmigan to eat?"

"Some ptarmigan? Why, there are plenty over there on the rocks at the top of those hills," replied the young man.

"Go there," grumbled the father-in-law, "go over there and try to catch some. Try to shoot them down with your arrows."

"Yes, yes," agreed the young man and he left immediately.

The father-in-law waited until his son-in-law was out of sight. Then he put on a long pair of waterproof boots made from seal skin and followed his son-in-law without the young man's knowledge. He was curious to see what was going to happen.

The son-in-law walked for a long time until he reached a rocky elevation. There he stopped, turned around and looked about everywhere. Having noticed nothing, he climbed to the top of the hill, never suspecting that his father-in-law, who was hidden by a rock, was watching his movements.

The young man remained standing for an instant, then put his bow down on the ground, threw his arrows to the earth and broke them with his feet. His father-in-law then saw him look all around, sit down, get up again and pace back and forth, all the while searching for something with his eyes. He saw him bend down suddenly and seize a small object. It was a stone with a surface as rough as a file, a very hard stone. The young man rubbed it on a rock but could not make it blunt.

The man then watched his son-in-law sit down and rub the stone against his boots, frequently checking the results of his efforts. When the soles were full of holes he started to work on the heels in the same fashion. From his hiding place the man cried, "My son-in-law is nothing but a liar, a big liar!"

The young man jumped up in surprise and looked around. He thought he had recognized his father-in-law's voice and wondered where he was. While turning his head from side to side in his search, he resumed his sitting position and tried to stick the pieces of arrows back together again with saliva. When this did not work he put his fingers into the holes of his boots, tore the leather and chewed the pieces in order to make a glue that he could use to repair the arrows. This did not work either so the young man had little choice but return to his wife's home.

When he arrived at their camp no one came out to greet him as was the custom when hunters returned. He stood motionless for a short time, holding his bow and broken arrows. Since no one emerged from the igloo, he knew that his misbehaviour had been discovered and he became afraid of his parents-in-law, particularly the father.

He decided to leave his bow in front of the igloo and run away. He was about to go when his mother-in-law stopped him by calling out: "Son-in-law! What are you doing? Come in. Have something to eat. After that you can leave."

The young man either did not hear, or hearing, did not wish to let on that the woman's voice was beckoning to him. He was afraid of her husband and so went away, barefooted.

The Bear and the Child

Three sisters, one of whom was soon to have a child, went picking fruit. While they were picking the fruit it began to rain and in searching for cover from the downpour, they discovered a deserted bear's cave. They squeezed themselves into the cave to wait until the rain stopped.

Suddenly they heard sounds outside and soon a huge bear was looking at them curiously through the entrance passageway. Two of the sisters managed to crawl through a narrow air hole and escape, but the third sister, who was pregnant, found herself cornered in the cave. The bear attacked and killed her.

When the bear tore open the woman's body she found a fully formed boy child in its mother's womb. The bear, a female, tossed the woman's body into a corner but decided to keep the child and raise it as her own.

For a long time the child lived snuggled close to the one he believed to be his mother. He learned to walk and to touch everything. One day he discovered some bones lying in a corner and comparing them with his naked body, he saw that they were similar to his own.

"Where did these bones come from, Mama?" he asked the bear.

"I don't know," she lied, "they were here when I came."

Later, when the child first ventured outdoors, the blinding light of the day struck him sharply in the face. As he grew older, however, he went outdoors more and more often, taking longer and longer walks. One day he killed his first game—a small mouse. He proudly took it home to show the bear who was so pleased and happy with him that from then on the boy always brought some game back to the cave.

In time the boy became skillful at hunting caribou. On one hunt he followed the river to the sea and while there he saw some creatures who, like himself, walked in an upright position. He returned home without having been seen by these people and questioned the bear.

"Who are these beings that look like me?"

The bear answered, "They are men and they will kill you. Do not return to that place."

One day the young boy said to the bear, "The animals have left this district. They have run away because of the odour from the bones, pieces of skin and dirt which litter our cave. Let's gather these things into a pile and burn them." This they did and from time to time during the warmth of the summer they would clean the area surrounding their cave.

But the young boy's curiosity was aroused. Despite the bear's warning, his hunting trips grew progressively longer as he made his way to the sea. Here he would crouch in hiding and observe the men, comparing his own body to theirs. Finally he left his hiding place and approached them.

The men were surprised to see this young, naked boy. When they questioned him and were told about his strange mother with many legs and huge teeth, they realized that he must be Ilviak's child, the son of their daughter who had been killed by a bear while pregnant.

Now the grandfather made the young boy a bow and arrow and taught him to use it. Then the grandfather told him to return to the bear's cave.

"When you arrive, hide your bow and when the bear is asleep, you will kill her with your arrows."

The young boy made the journey back to the cave, taking no game. He explained to the bear that he could find no game because the surroundings of the cave smelled badly and he suggested that the next day they make a fire and burn the garbage. On the morrow the boy stirred the flames and fed them with willows while the bear stretched out to sleep in the warmth. She asked the boy to delouse her and as he did so she fell asleep. Taking advantage of this situation, the boy went to get his bow. As he bent the bow to send the arrow toward the bear, the huge beast shook herself and awoke.

She was furious and howled with anger, "What are you doing? I have forbidden you to use a bow and arrow!" The bear chased the boy around and around the blazing fire until, with one sudden leap, the boy jumped over the fire and shot his arrow, killing the bear.

The boy had killed the one he had long believed to be his mother and so he went to live with the men by the sea. It is said that he was very strong and lithe, and that in games and in hunting no child his age could outdo him.

The Dog and the Young Girl

A long time ago illness struck several families who were living together. The people died in large numbers. Among the victims was an old couple. Their young daughter did not die but was left alone in the world with her dog.

The other survivors, fearful of the tragedy that had struck down their companions, left the area, thus abandoning the young orphan. She found herself stripped of all aid and left with only her dog—two lonely beings in an empty land.

Not knowing what to do the girl and her dog also left the settlement. Wandering about on their own they soon became lost, far from any place of habitation. But eventually they came upon an igloo, a very small one which they could use as a shelter.

Once installed in their igloo the girl took her place by the stone lamp. Across from her, on the far side of the room, she prepared a bed for the dog. Here they would remain.

During the days that followed, when the weather was pleasant and there was no danger of freezing, the two of them went hunting for small game. Ptarmigan, marmots and small birds were caught for food. Without weapons they had to make do with what they could catch. Larger animals such as caribou had to be forgotten. In this manner the girl and her dog managed to survive in the bleak frozen desert.

One night the dog became ill. Apparently he had come down with a fever.

The perspiration from his body froze his fur, covering him with frost and icicles. On awakening the girl found her dog in a pitiful state. What had happened to him? What should she do? She trembled as she thought that he could be very sick and might well die. In desperation she made the dog get up onto her bed where she tried to dry his hair. Despite everything she tried, the dog's condition worsened. He looked as if he were freezing to death.

All of a sudden the dog roused himself and spoke in a sad, discouraging voice. "Tomorrow a white bear will come to get you. He wants you for his wife." With those words the dog fell into a deep sleep.

The next day, somewhat refreshed from his rest, the dog spoke once more. "Look often toward the north. It is from there that the white bear will come." Several times during the day the girl left the igloo to scan the northern horizon. Late in the day the girl returned to the igloo saying, "I can see him!"

Hearing this news the dog told her to go and prepare the necessary food for the visitor. Quickly she prepared everything and then went outside to view the approach of the bear. Hastily she retreated to the igloo telling the dog as she did so that the visitor would soon arrive. Without hesitation the dog gave further directions. "Seat yourself near the door. When the bear has finished eating he will tell you that he wants you. Pretend that you are listening closely. Then when I wink, rush outside!"

The dog had barely finished speaking when the bear entered. The girl proceeded to serve the food and then went and sat by the door. As soon as he had finished eating, the bear spoke.

"I have come to take the young girl for my wife."

The dog replied, "If you take her what will become of me? She is the only one who can hunt for me in this place where no one else lives."

"If necessary I shall kill you but the girl comes with me," answered the bear.

At that moment the dog winked and upon seeing this signal the girl fled the igloo. Once outside she remained near the entrance listening to the noise of the fight that now took place. As soon as the sounds were silenced she glanced inside. Her first thoughts were that her dog, who had been so weakened by his strange illness, would be dead. To her surprise, the dog was alive! He had killed the bear.

The girl and her dog were very happy. Not only was there now plenty of bear meat to eat but better yet, the dog returned to good health. Soon his coat was gleaming as before. In the days that followed the two of them resumed their daily routine of going for walks and catching those small animals that were available to them.

Sometime thereafter, this pleasant interlude was broken by the return of the dog's illness. His coat lost its sheen. Fever and loss of weight combined to reduce him to a weakened condition indeed. Once more his companion tried to comfort and care for him. The dog's sickness only became worse. He was becoming little more than skin and bones.

At his lowest ebb, the dog spoke. "Two white bears will come to get you. They will arrive from the north tomorrow. You must make them something to eat and then follow my directions as before."

The next day the girl did as she was told. Everything was in readiness when the bears entered the igloo. The meal was laid out on the table before them. While they were eating, the girl quietly went to sit by the door.

When the meal was over, one of the bears spoke. "We have come to get the girl."

Without bothering to lift his head the dog replied, "If you take her what will become of me? She is the only companion that I have in this empty land."

"It doesn't matter," answered the other bear. "We shall take her even if it means killing you and since there are two of us we expect no trouble."

At this reply, the dog glanced over at the girl and winked. Immediately she ran outside. A great fight then broke out between the bears and the dog. For what seemed a long time the battle raged. Initially, the girl could hear her companion's barking but soon the noise of the struggle made it impossible to tell just what was taking place. The girl waited.

When all was still the girl poked her head inside the igloo to see what the outcome of the fight had been. To her amazement both bears were dead! There stood her dog, the victor a second time. Great was their elation. The dog recovered his health and the supply of fresh meat was such as they had never known before.

The girl now understood the reasons for her dog's periodic illness. Whenever he sensed danger he intentionally lost weight in order to become lean and tough. Although he appeared to be in extremely poor condition, he was actually in fighting trim.

Their normal existence resumed. When it became necessary, ptarmigan and marmots were caught for food. The weather was fine. The girl and her dog were happy. Unfortunately, their joy did not last; the dog became seriously ill once again.

This time the girl knew what to expect. Some danger was about to befall them. In vain she tried to nurse her companion back to good health. Nothing seemed to work. Death appeared to be a certainty. When the end seemed near the dog gathered what little strength he had and spoke to the girl.

"Three bears will come for you tomorrow. In my weakened condition I do not know if I shall be able to protect you. I shall try. You and I have been through much misery together. Ever since the people abandoned us like so much rubbish we have had to struggle for our existence. One bear, two bears, I could handle. Three bears, I do not know, but I cannot leave you now." With those words he fell asleep.

The girl followed the same procedures as before. The meal was prepared. Three bears arrived and while they were eating the girl stationed herself by the door. Meanwhile the dog curled up in the corner pretending to be asleep.

The bears were full of confidence. They lingered over their meal. There was lots of time. When they had finished, they announced that they had come for the girl. At this remark the dog protested.

"What about me? You cannot leave me here by myself. I need the help of my companion."

"That is no concern of ours," replied the bears. "There are three of us and we shall kill you and then take the girl."

Scrambling to his feet, the dog signalled the girl. Quickly, she ran out the door. "What chance does my poor dog have this time?" wondered the girl.

The battle that followed raged on and on. Finally it was over. Hardly daring to look inside, the girl cautiously entered the igloo.

What should she see but the three bears lying dead on the floor! She could not believe her eyes. Her dog had fought and won his greatest fight. Never again would danger strike at the hearts of these two lonely creatures. They would live peacefully and quietly in their wilderness home until the end of their lives.

Design and Production by David Shaw